Where
Resident
Aliens
Live

Stanley Hauerwas
William H. Willimon

Where Resident Aliens Live

Exercises for Christian Practice

Abingdon Press
Nashville

WHERE RESIDENT ALIENS LIVE:
EXERCISES FOR CHRISTIAN PRACTICE

Copyright © *1996 by Abingdon Press*

This book is printed on acid-free, recycled paper.

ISBN 0-687-01605-3

Unless otherwise noted, Scripture quotations are from the New Revised Standard Version Bible. Copyright 1989 by the Division of Christian Education of the National Council of the Churches of Christ in the USA. Used by permission.

Thomas E. Ricks, " 'New' Marines Illustrate Growing Gap Between Military and Society" in *The Wall Street Journal,* Thursday July 27, 1995. Reprinted by permission of *The Wall Street Journal,* © 1995 Dow Jones & Company, Inc. All Rights Reserved Worldwide.

Pages 113-118 are from an "Interview." *The Door* (May/June 1993), pp. 249-64. Reprinted by permission.

96 97 98 99 00 01 02 03 04 05—10 9 8 7 6 5 4 3 2 1

To Bishop Kenneth Carder

PREFACE

We worry about sequels. But so many have read *Resident Aliens,* then asked us questions, and wanted clarification of this or that point. We attempt to answer some of those questions. As well we answer some of the criticism that is aimed at resident aliens. We have reprinted some of the criticism in this book so that the reader who does not read reviews will have some sense of the reactions to resident aliens.

We owe many people debts, and we try to indicate a few of these in the book itself. We are thrilled by the many Christians who lead lives more faithful than ours who tell us that *Resident Aliens* was a godsend to them. They make us possible.

We are indebted to Kelley Johnson, a good Roman Catholic, for reading and criticizing the book for us. She made invaluable suggestions.

We dedicate this book to Kenneth Carder—for his courage and his humility.

CONTENTS

The medium for being a Christian has been shifted from existence and the ethical to the intellectual, the metaphysical, the imaginary; a more or less theatrical relationship has been introduced between thinking Christianity and being Christian — and thus being a Christian has been abolished.
    —*Søren Kierkegaard, "Armed Neutrality"*[1]

CHAPTER ONE

Resident Aliens Among Us

On Being a Success When We Did Not Intend to Be

Resident Aliens is a success. Well over fifty thousand people have bought copies of a book that a critic said "was a death-wish for the church." Depending upon one's definition of *success*, the sales of *Resident Aliens* may or may not be great news. Before writing *Resident Aliens*, Will told Stanley that he was going to make him famous; that is, he was going to drag Stanley's work out of the rarified realm of "serious scholarship" where it had been causing a stir mainly among academics, and introduce the church to Hauerwas in words of one syllable.

Stanley is now famous, and the rarified academy is taking more notice.

But Stanley is uncertain how to react to his new

Stanley Hauerwas hates liberalism. He hates liberal theology, liberal ethics, liberal churches, liberal politics, liberal economics, and liberal democracy. He uses military terms . . . to signal that he is part of a great battle against liberalism, waged on behalf of virtue, character and pacifism. His weapons in this battle are narrative theology and postmodern philosophy (plus some bluster). . . . [But] Christianity has a liberal element at its core.[1]
—Max Stackhouse

11

fame. Stanley has the notion that, if the church were really to live the faith as advocated by *Resident Aliens*, it would be a considerably smaller church. The success of this book suggests that the number of "aliens," or those who have the potential of becoming so, is considerably larger than Stanley thought.

Will thinks that, if Stanley is not offending someone, if half the room is not walking out in anger after his lecture, then Stanley thinks that he has said something unfaithful. Stanley is embarrassed that so many people read the book and agreed with it.

The response to that book is similar to the way Paul Ramsey felt after he wrote his famous essay "On a Dignified Death." Ramsey suddenly found that essay celebrated by a new breed called "thanatologists." The thanatologists had been inspired by Kübler-Ross's famous book *On Death and Dying*, which suggested that people go through various stages when they die. They begin in denial, move to anger, try to defeat death through bargaining, proceed to apathy, and finally reaching an acceptance of good death. Ramsey did not want his work put to that use. Accordingly, he wrote a later essay entitled "On the Indignity of a Dignified Death."

Like Ramsey, we are suspicious of "success" because if resident aliens are close to being right, agreeing with them should entail much pain. We all live in one way or another in this society as liberals. So to understand what we were trying to do in *Resident Aliens* puts us at odds with ourselves. That includes Willimon and Hauerwas. If you are to become a resident alien, it will require pain that will not necessarily make you a friend of yourself and all the other liberals who are beneficiaries of the status quo.

But at the same time we believe that many have responded positively to becoming resident aliens exactly because it helps us deal with the pain which we unfortunately and erroneously call "freedom." For example, a Baptist pastor in Atlanta stood before his board of deacons and told them, "If you want to be another thousand-member Baptist church in Atlanta, then go ahead. Almost any Baptist church in Atlanta can do that. However, if that's the kind of church you want to be, then you must do it without me."

He told them that he had no pastoral interest in becoming a "success," as so many other churches defined that term. When asked what he wanted, he told them that he wanted their church to be a church that was formed by peculiarly Christian convictions, that articulated a cost of discipleship and sought out those few who wanted to pay the price—that sort of church.

His deacons wanted to hear more. He had them all read *Resident Aliens* on a deacons' retreat that fall. They reinvisioned their church, made plans for themselves on the basis of rediscovered Christian practices, and promised to share this vision with the rest of their congregation.

They are at it again. The prophets Hauerwas and Willimon have issued yet another indictment of contemporary Christian life and have sounded yet another call for church renewal and faithfulness. Hauerwas and Willimon declare that the old world of a shared Christian piety "has ended and a new world is being born" (p. 146). In this new secular world "paganism is the air we breathe, the water we drink. It captures us, it converts our young, it subverts the church" (p. 151).[2]
—Rebekah Miles-Deloney

"Trouble is," said this young pastor as he told us this story, "I think we are still going to be that thousand-member Baptist church! We keep raising our requirements, keep asking people to do more, and still they come. Many in the world know that something is not right, and they are eager for a church that knows how to name their pain and has a vision of a better way."

We believe that the main reason why many read and appreciate *Resident Aliens* is that it is not original with us. The book is merely sounding a chord in a growing symphony to which many have contributed. When one can count Lesslie Newbigin, George Lindbeck, Will Campbell, William Stringfellow, John Milbank, and Karl Barth among a book's contributors, one is obviously part of a large, expansive movement headed somewhere interesting. Indeed, by naming peculiar Christians as resident aliens, we discovered friends we did not know we had.

Known by the Friends We Keep

We were introduced to new friends like those Christian communitarians in Oregon and California. They contacted Stanley, saying, "We're trying to live the faith you only talk about in your book. Come see us." Stanley did, and there he found a group that has established a half dozen communities around the West where Christians come together to live, to share their material resources, together raise their children, support their marriages, and to experiment with radical Christian community. We found their church to be scary. What if resident aliens are not merely the idle dream of a couple of professors, but are a realistic possibility among those who take seriously the gospel? That's scary.

Will also recalls fondly the woman who came up to him at a meeting of Episcopalians in Kentucky, saying, "Hi, I'm Gladys."

"Gladys?" he asked.

"Gladys! Gladys in the book," she said. Then Will remembered dear Gladys in *Resident Aliens* (chapter 6).

"I had just returned from a Vestry Meeting, still seething. I was lying in bed, reading while my husband slept. I read about Gladys and the day-care center. I slapped my husband, saying 'Look! Here I am in this book! They're writing about me.' "

She explained that earlier at the meeting of the Vestry, the youth minister had given a glowing report on the visit of the youth to DisneyWorld. After the report, this "Gladys II" asked, "What does taking the youth to DisneyWorld have to do with youth ministry?"

With some defensiveness in his voice, the minister explained that this was "to build community among our youth group."

"They can build community right here in Louisville," said Gladys II. "I can't see the point of taking a group of privileged, affluent youth to DisneyWorld. They've already been there and done that."

The minister continued to defend the trip, with a tone of growing defensiveness in his voice. "Our kids don't know each other. Community is important."

"*Christian* community is important," rebutted Gladys II. "Taking a group of spoiled, privileged kids to a place like DisneyWorld where all they'll do is romp in a capitalist playground for four days, bringing out all of their worst tendencies, is a waste of time for the church as far as I am concerned."

Gladys II said, "At that point, they started yelling at me."

We remember Gladys II, a resident alien, with love.

Furthermore, the very way in which the book was written was meant to embody something of its claims. We wrote the book together. Stanley kids Will, saying that Will has never had an unpublished thought—and most of the good ones are Hauerwas's. Will's retort is that nobody would have heard any of Stanley's thoughts had it not been for Will's superior syntax.

The test of a good community, even one as small as two friends, is that its members have been talking together so much and for so long that they no longer remember whose thought belongs to whom. We think that's the community the church aspires to be.

So when someone asks, "Where are all the great prophets of our time?" you can respond that the whole notion of "great prophets of our time" shows a misunderstanding of prophecy. Prophecy is not the activity of the lone, unique genius or the courageous social critic. Prophecy is a communal achievement. Christian social criticism is secondary to our primary activity of church formation. Prophets—like that Baptist preacher in Atlanta, like those Christian disciples in California and Oregon, like Gladys II in Kentucky—direct our attention to the significance of the lives of the faithful. Their testimony to the gospel is no lone, heroic achievement. What makes faithful prophecy is its linkage to the essential practices of the church. In speaking to the church, these prophets speak to as much "world" as most of us ever see. Their truthfulness keeps the church as the church.

The Glory of the Ordinary

You will note that resident aliens are utterly "ordinary," as the world judges these things. We are surprised when many persons say, "Where in the world is this church which you describe?" Or "The church you want doesn't exist." We thought we had bent over backward, in our illustrations and narratives in *Resident Aliens,* to use examples that were ordinary, local, and typical, so as to underscore that the sort of prophetic church we had in mind already exists, at least in glimpses.

Of course nothing, as has often been observed, is more extraordinary than common sense. So the ordinary people we celebrate are in quite interesting ways extraordinary. One of the difficulties, however, of the extraordinary nature of their faithfulness is that when they and those who admire them lack the means to name why their lives are so important, they lose their significance. So in many ways our book is an attempt to narrate the ordinary in a way that will help us preserve the extraordinary significance of the lives we hold up. That is why *Resident Aliens,* as well as this book, is an ongoing attempt to teach us how to speak well as Christians. Nothing is more important than having Christian speech work in a way that it determines who we are.

For example, we do not as Christians call one another *heroic.* Rather, we call one another *faithful.* Some of those faithful witnesses we even learn to describe as *saints.* So nothing is more important than learning to speak well so that the significance of the lives God has given us is not lost for the upbuilding of the church.

That is why it is so important that the account of the church we provide not be described as "unrealistic" or "idealistic" or "sectarian." These responses are merely some of the many means of avoiding conversion and defending ourselves against the possibility that God not only calls us toward but enables us to embody more than present ecclesial arrangements.

We are compelled to name *where* resident aliens live. This book signifies our response to those who wondered, "Where is this church of which you speak?" The heart of this present book is found in the examples we use. These examples are meant to serve as reminders that the church has not been forsaken by God. The church is still visible, if we take the trouble to look for it in the right places. We still have practices in place, in your church and ours, which can be resources for faithful renewal. But it is crucial that they be understood as practices and not simply as "beliefs." Finally, it is a matter of truth, and the truth that is gospel is known only through practices such as preaching, baptism, eucharist—in short, *worship*.

> *Despite its strong points, though, this book remains a superficial examination of the problem. Its anecdotal style is initially engaging but ultimately left me dissatisfied. It is reminiscent of what is wrong with the storytelling method of preaching that is so popular today. The stories help us to pay attention but offer no substance. . . . the examples are catchy but wither for a lack of depth and analysis. . . . The authors are intent on bashing the Niebuhr brothers for urging the church to become politically involved. While there is room for criticism, the authors offer no substantive alternative. . . .*

The authors lift up the pre-Constantinian church as an example, but they fail to address the fact that those churches reflected in the biblical story were much more diverse than are current North American churches. The churches of our age tend to be homogeneous. The early church wrestled with the political issues in a "down-home" way—slaves and masters, rich and poor, Greek and Jew all worshipped and shared life together in the early church. The early church was forced to deal with political issues by the very diversity of its membership. We are lucky if 5% of our churches reflect any kind of diversity, a diversity that usually calls churches to make the kind of stand against the culture that the authors want. For the church to be the colony that the authors wish, we will have to find a way to enable our congregations to become more diverse. . . . They offer no help on this issue.

This book is a good beginning [but]. . . . What does it mean to be a "resident alien?"[3]

—Nibs Stroupe

As James Edwards has observed in his forthcoming book, *The Plain Sense of Things: The Fate of Religion in an Age of Values*, once religion becomes a matter of belief we think it natural to raise questions of whether those beliefs are as true and/or as useful as some other beliefs that we have before us. Once the question is raised in such terms, it does not matter much what the answer turns out to be in a given dispute. In other words, "once religious beliefs start to compete with other beliefs, then religious believers are—and will know themselves to be—managers of values; they too are denizens of the mall, selling and shopping and buying alongside the rest of us."

By focusing on practices we are trying to find ways to help one another resist the tendency for Christianity to become a matter of belief, of values. We are trying in short to help you rediscover the nonvoluntary character of what it means to be a member of the church of Jesus Christ. Such a view obviously flies in the face of the assumption that the church is a voluntary agency of like-minded individuals. Yet we believe that Christians must find the means to resist such construals of the church if the world is to discover the truth of the narrative that makes credible the practices we call "church."

We will tell even more stories, give more instances of fidelity, offer more examples of a church in which ordinary people are called to be saints. We have been blessed with much mail, wonderful testimonials and stories from those who have actually seen what we professors only describe. We offer these examples because we believe that the contemporary church suffers from a lack of political imagination. One reason why the church always focused upon the stories of the saints and the martyrs was to enlarge our imagination. No conversion or growth is possible without imagination.

One of the saints appealing to us is Karl Barth. We cut our theological teeth on Barth. He saved us from liberal Protestant assumptions that one has to translate Christian language in order to have it heard. Rather, Barth helped us realize that if the language is doing no work, the problem is in the church and not in the language. So Barth forces us to recognize the integrity of the speech that Christians have been given. Unfortunately we find Barth's own ecclesiology rather deficient.

That may seem an odd criticism for a Christian who was able to stand against the Nazis in the name of the gospel. Unfortunately, Barth did not seem to have a way to run that stance into an account of the practices needed to sustain the church beyond its confrontation with the Nazis.

Barth had no examples of such a church. The Reformed Church in Switzerland was his primary example, and it was insufficient because it was little more than a would-be national club, a social convention. We all need more examples to have a sense of what it would mean for the church to be the church. Catholicism always attracted Barth, we suspect, exactly because he knew he needed such examples. So part of our task is to hold up exemplification of Barth's theology better than Barth could provide for himself.

We are admittedly not clear about the internal processes of the church that God is birthing in our midst. That is, we do not know the organizational and institutional details. There is no ideal church "back there" that we believe we ought to imitate. Indeed, one of the great forms of unfaithfulness is trying to make the "success" of one time a guarantee for a future time. Things keep changing. You can never stay the same. We believe we have only just begun exploring what the faithful church should look like.

Some have asked us, "Which form of the church has most influenced your thinking about the church?" Stanley has been deeply influenced by John Howard Yoder and the Mennonites. Will wrote his senior religion thesis at Wofford College on "The Anabaptist View of the Church."

Yet Stanley also experienced vital Catholic sacramental piety while he was on the faculty at Notre Dame. Surely one reason why so many Episcopalians and Lutherans like the image of resident aliens is that they hear voiced a sacramentalism as high as their own. The eucharistic prayer is one of the most distinctive practices.

One can understand why someone might wonder where we get our ecclesiology. After all, we are both United Methodists, in varying degrees of happiness. Mainstream United Methodism is about as far from some of the views of resident aliens as night is from day. Yet in its stress on sanctification, on the importance of the practical, practiced embodiment of the faith by the laity, we thought that our resident aliens are a very Methodist people.

When asked, "What church do you have in mind?" Will might refer to the African American church he remembers in South Carolina before and during the days of the civil rights movement. Here was a church that knew that it lived as strangers in a strange land, that had no illusions about the wider culture, that knew that it needed to gather on Sunday and protect its children. White supremacists knew what they were doing when in the 1960s they bombed and burned many of these churches. The fidelity of these churches was known by the folk whom they produced (one of them named Martin Luther King), and they were known as enemies of everything for which the white supremacists stood.

Yet Will also realizes belatedly that he is also deeply influenced by campus ministry. At Duke, as on nearly any campus, the Christian groups that thrive are those who stress the importance of the group, the centrality of equipping the saints (Ephesians 5:21-33), the skills needed for resistance.

So when Will meets with a group of Lutherans on our campus, Lutherans meeting at 9:00 P.M. in the chapel for eucharist, he says, "When you left Des Moines, you probably thought that Lutherans were in charge of something. With a large organ, a full parking lot on Sunday, you probably thought that your church was socially significant. But you came here to the university, and you realized that we are out to kill Lutherans. Don't take it personally; we treat Catholics and Jews the same way. The university hopes to make you a lot less Lutheran than you were when you came here.

"By faith Abraham obeyed when he was called to set out for a place that he was to receive as an inheritance; and he set out, not knowing where he was going. . . . He looked forward to the city that has foundations, whose architect and builder is God."
—Hebrews 11:8, 10

"So you learned that, if you were going to survive as a Lutheran, you must get in a group, you must gather every week, you must do Lutheran things, sing Lutheran songs, and eat Lutheran food. I say that you are the wave of the future. More than your church in Des Moines knows it, it looks a lot like you. I believe (you heard it here first) that you are the church of tomorrow. The skills and practices you are learning here in your Lutheran campus ministry group will be immediately transferable back to Des Moines. More than they know it back in Des Moines, they are in the same boat."

We have the impression that younger pastors and laity, say those under forty, prefer resident aliens more than do older pastors and laity. It is not only a matter that many of the older generation, having fought, bled, and died for openness, affirmation, and inclusiveness of everything that moves, find our call for a distinctive church to be alarming, but it is also that the younger generation seems to have had more experiences which have led them to give up on the accommodationist project and to be eager for something more adequate to the task.

On Not Feeling at Home

Because one of us is from South Carolina and the other is from Texas, we have never felt particularly at home in a place like the university. The one from Texas feels out of place even in Durham. He thinks Southern civility one of the most calculated forms of cruelty ever produced.

The image of resident aliens means in a possibly offensive way that American Christians need to stop feeling at home. We agree with Lesslie Newbigin that today's Western church ought to feel like missionaries in the very culture we thought we had devised. American Christians thought that we had created, through our Constitution, a culture in which people were at last safe to be Christians.

That was a mistake. The very notion that we Christians could ever feel at home in this culture or any other was criticized by Hugo of St. Victor: "The man who finds his homeland sweet is still a tender beginner; he to whom every soil is as his native one is already strong;

but he is perfect to whom the entire world is a foreign place." By being adopted to be part of a journey called discipleship, Christians are permanently ill at ease in the world.

Wise Malcolm Muggeridge prayed that "the only ultimate disaster that can befall us is to feel ourselves to be at home here on earth. As long as we are aliens we cannot forget our true homeland which is that other kingdom You proclaimed."

Constantinianism, which attempted through force of the state to make the world into the kingdom, which attempted to make the worship of God unavoidable, which attempted to make Christian convictions available to all without conversion or transformation, was an ill-conceived project that has at last died of its own deceit. As Stanley has said, "It is unclear who started looking like whom first, whether Southern Baptist pastors started looking like Texas politicians, or Texas politicians started looking like Southern Baptist pastors."

Because we grew up in mainline Protestantism, we know that project well. American mainline Protestants hoped to be so nice, hoped to remake the gospel into something so self-evident and obvious, that the world would think that it was already Christian without having to die and be reborn. Fortunately, now that that project seems to be in its death throes, on the basis of membership statistics alone, many are now ready to let go of that deceit and to embrace their new status as sojourners. America, for any of its strengths and blessings, is not God's salvation.

The laity appear to prefer resident aliens more readily than do clergy. We think that's because the laity have gotten the news that, as Christians, we are in some kind of fight. They seemed to resonate with the claim that, rather than send resolutions to Congress, a more realistic political act on the part of the church would be to serve the world by being the church.

Some have accused us of a kind of hypocrisy, that we continue to feed off of the strengths of the residual Christianity that bores us, at the same time fiercely criticizing the Christianity that made us possible. We bite the ecclesial hand that feeds us. We do not deny this accusation. We confess that we are both probably more residual, compromised Christians than we ought to be. Constantinianism is a hard habit to break. But why should we turn the deficiencies of our own lives into justification for the way Christians can and should live?

Perhaps we are being self-deceptive, but we like to think of ourselves as missionaries in the contemporary university. There may come a day when the university wakes up and discovers how at odds we are with its dominant modes of thought and action. Stanley keeps saying that he hopes that Will will one day preach the gospel so clearly in Duke Chapel, so vividly and compellingly, that the university administration will say, "Are we crazy for

> *Stanley Hauerwas and William Willimon see the church as resident alien. . . . Unfortunately, however, this accent is inappropriate for the mainline churches. . . . Hauerwas and Willimon . . . suggest that "the church is a colony, an island of one culture in the middle of another" (p. 12); that implies that the church is to American society what the missionary compound once was to Chinese culture. Curiously, such a view virtually describes, unwittingly to be sure, the megachurches . . . a world within a world.[4]*
> —Leander Keck

paying the salary of a subversive like this? This guy is against everything we believe in."

That has not happened—yet. But, as Jesus told his disciples after he had just about given up hope for the salvation of the rich young man (Luke 18:27), with God, anything is possible—even the salvation of educated, rich, arrogant, and self-sufficient people like us.

As missionaries to the university, we believe that we have the joyful task of announcing to the university the gospel's interesting claims about the world, not the least of which is that the world is *created*. Think of *Resident Aliens* as a manual for missionaries who have been on furlough for the longest time but now are ready to go back into the fray.

• • •

He came to the chapel rather regularly, throughout his first couple of years at the university. One of the first times that Will talked with him, he told Will that his mother had him read *Resident Aliens*. "I liked the book, but I don't know many Christians that it fits."

Later, Will was surprised to receive a call from him early one Monday morning.

"Dr. Willimon, are you up yet?" a hoarse, tense young voice asked.

"Yes."

"I need to see you right away. I've had a terrible night and need to talk."

"I'll meet you at the Chapel in thirty minutes," Will said.

Upon arriving at the back door of the Chapel, the student greeted Will and fell into his arms in tears.

"What's happened?" Will asked.

"It's terrible. I've had the worst night of my life. Last night, after the fraternity meeting, as usual, we had a time when we just sit around and talk about what we did over the weekend. This weekend, during a party we had on Saturday, I went upstairs to get something from a brother's room and walked in on a couple who were, well, 'in the act.'

"I immediately closed the door and went back downstairs, saying nothing. Well, when we came to the time for sharing at the end of the meeting, after a couple of the brothers shared what they did over the weekend, one of the group said, 'I understand that Mr. Christian got a real eye-full last night.'

"With that, they all began to laugh. Not a good, friendly laugh; it was cold, cruel, mean laughter. They were all laughing, all saying things like, 'You won't see nothin' like that in church!' and 'Better go confess it to the priest,' and stuff like that.

"I tried to recover, tried to say something light, but I couldn't. They hate me! They were serious. I walked out of the meeting and stood outside and wept. I've never been treated like that in my life."

Will said something like, "That's amazing. And you're not the greatest Christian in the whole world, are you? And yet, just one person running around loose who can say, No! is a threat to everyone else, has to be put down, ridiculed, savaged into silence. This campus may make a Christian out of you, despite yourself!"

In encountering the witness of that young resident alien, forgive the two of us for feeling a bit of pride at our success.

CHAPTER TWO

Interpreting the Present Time

On Being Surrounded

"Do you think that I have come to bring peace to the earth? No, I tell you, but rather division! From now on five in one household will be divided, three against two and two against three; they will be divided:

father against son
 and son against father,
mother against daughter
 and daughter against mother,
mother-in-law against her
  daughter-in-law
 and daughter-in-law against
  mother-in-law. . . .

Why do you not know how to interpret the present time?" (Luke 12:51-53, 56)

The accusation that we are "sectarians" strikes us as especially strange. To our surprise, some assert that resident alien Christians are called to withdraw from the world. Retreat. This accusation is surprising because both of us work at a large, secular university. A university is not a monastery. But also this seems to us an odd misreading of the imagination that is required to be resident aliens. We are not asking Christians to withdraw from the world but rather to recognize that we are surrounded. To where could we possibly withdraw? Moreover, in such a world it would be dangerous indeed for us "to circle the wagons," to cower behind the barricades, as if the task of the church is to try to protect itself from the world.

Rather, we believe that if Christians live faithfully, the world will seek protection from the church. The task of the church is not to retreat into its own enclave but to keep heading further out despite the dangers. Indeed, the very fact that we keep pursuing our mission means that we necessarily create dangers that otherwise would not be there if we had stayed home.

We think that we're ill prepared for the journey that God has made for us in our day. We live in a world that is dangerous to the church because of our church's self-deception that Christianity has tamed the world. For example, the assumption that this is a Christian civilization is dangerous because it deludes us into thinking that we now have no enemy. In a church that has now made peace with the world, we are deluded into thinking that our task is to smooth out the rough edges of a project long ago begun to make the world safe for the church.

As a result, the presumption is that the church is all right; we need only make the world a bit better. Our claim is that such an account is deeply deceptive, has always been deeply deceptive, but is peculiarly deceptive in these times between the times. As Stanley has said in *After Christendom*, this is an awkward age. It is awkward because an old world is dying and it's not yet clear what the new world is to look like. The old world that is dying is the world of mainstream Protestant Christianity with its presumption that America is somehow a nation unlike other nations because it is based on Christian presuppositions. "Based on Christian pre-suppositions" usually means that we live in a democratic culture that is intrinsically supportive of what it means to be a Christian. We are calling that into question.

In an ecclesial atmosphere worried about declining church membership and Christian identity, this book is likely to be provocative and popular but not adequate to reforming ministry to the present world. Our problem, it argues, is as simple as it is complex: we have failed to be the church we were called to be; and the solution, sounded through the book with liturgical consistency, is "let the church be the church." . . . . There's nothing new here for the world to see; the aim seems to be to keep that faithful, and so impress the hungry world that it will eagerly come to the church's table. This is a first-century strategy for awaiting an imminent messianic return. But even Paul's church knew that "walking in the Spirit" meant more than Christians looking out for their own purity. It also meant dangerous conversation in public forums to proclaim Good News and persuade others, through debate and dialogue in public language, of the gospel truth. . . . What the book fails to address—and, in fact, dismisses implicitly as "Constantinianism"—is the consequence of legitimate theology, which sees God at work outside the colony's confines through voices and structures that are woven into a pluralistic, global reality. In this book, "the world has ended," and what remains is a hostile environment which is fundamentally false; there is no room for dialogue here, only conversion. Thus the Christianity promoted by the book is unblushingly imperialistic, appropriate to the language of divine kingship. But the realm of God's rule is not the world but the church, this "commonwealth of heaven." Thus there is a little room for imagining God leaving the ecclesial throne to go before God's people into a painful, suffering world.

There is little guidance here for engaging other truth claims, for establishing conversation with non-Christian people of belief. There is no listening here for God's voice in another language than that of the church. The result is a book that bears a tone of arrogant simplicity. . . . One would suspect . . . in the book, that religious educators would be prime culprits in the so-called accommodationist sin. . . . Thoughtfulness has given way to diatribe. There is truth here, important for us to take notice; but despite the claims, it's not all here and not all that's here rings true.[1]

—David C. Hester

William Stringfellow tells of leading a Bible study on the Acts of the Apostles in the little Episcopal church on Block Island. Because all of the material available had been produced by professional Christian educators, Stringfellow said he knew that "the stuff was theologically untrustworthy." So he decided to spend the ten sessions reading and talking about Acts with the group of eleven- and twelve-year-olds. At the end of the series, Stringfellow asked the students whether there was any reason for the church to be on Block Island, in view of what the class had discovered the church to be from reading in Acts. They were unanimous, some rather strenuous, in the opinion that, because the community as a whole acted so much like the church, there was no special cause to have a separate institution on the island that professed the name *church*.[2]

Christian educators, many of whom have spent their entire ministry helping Christians to adjust to the surrounding culture, are among the chief culprits in our current situation. Implicit in their accommodation is the assumption that it is possible to be the church without conflict. You will note that our conviction is to remind Christians that we are in a fight. Do not make your practices relevant to the prevailing language. Do not withdraw, but rather engage the enemy.

For example, when Christians were the enemy of the Roman Empire, they knew who their enemy was. The enemy was "out there." The language of the "powers," so prominent in the New Testament as the embodiment of evil, made real sense. Christ had defeated those powers. But exactly because they were defeated, they were all the more awesome in their terror. Once Christians, however, had made peace with Rome they began to think that salvation had to do with their inner life. Accordingly, satisfaction theories of the atonement became determinative for the church's christology. Such theories certainly have resonances in the New Testament, but when they are divorced from the church's sense that we are in a cosmic battle, we lose the ability to fight the war.

One of the marks of the church's extraordinary accommodation in our time is that Christians now believe that we have no enemy. Indeed, the presumption is that if there were an enemy, it would probably be our passions. That is why contemporary Christians erroneously focus so much on sex, because they think that lacking any external threat, the threat must come from within, and that usually has to do with sexual desires. So the church struggles to help us to control our passions, which we mistakenly assume are internal because we now have no external threat to our well-being. Of course, our inner war becomes externalized because we Christians think that we are so screwed up sexually due to the world's being so screwed up sexually. So we attack advertising, and we blame Calvin Klein and Beneton for the overt sexuality and kiddieporn of their ads. We call for family values. If only we were in charge of the world!

We hope thereby to protect ourselves from our deepest desires. Our fixation on the "inner" occurs because Christians have lost a sense of our true enemy.

Learning to Recognize Our Enemies Before We Try to Love Them

Nothing is more important than knowing our enemy. Indeed, the first task of the church is to teach us who is our enemy. Today the enemy is insufficiently identified as ourselves. The church must name the enemy as that manner of life that domesticates us by convincing us that the enemy is within. We are therefore deeply sympathetic with the apocalyptic imagery of the New Testament, which helps us understand that the threat to the church is not just war, hunger, and injustice to the poor. All of these evils are identified by the New Testament as adversaries, but they are not *the* enemy. These are merely the miseries that are brought to us by the nations and empires that derive their authority from promising to do good for us if we will behave as cooperative citizens. It is the church's task to expose the pretensions of those nations and empires as the enemy.

Particularly important in this respect is the church's ability to show the connection between the threat that comes from nations and empires and the concentration on sex as the enemy. We certainly agree that sexual questions are important for the church, but they are important as part of the discipline necessary for the church to be an army capable of confronting nations and empires. Sex is used in a capitalist economy as anesthesia and tranquilizer, so it is not without its dangers. The danger is that we fail to understand how the enemy uses sex to capture us.

Some shake their heads, after hearing about resident aliens, and worry about a "new sectarianism," or "resurgent tribalism," or a call for the church to become "a Christian ghetto." Yet who taught us that *sect, tribe,* and *ghetto* are bad words?

The same folk who arrived on this continent and, upon finding that people already lived here, told them, "We are going to give you the privilege to get out of your tribe and move into the modern, democratic world. We will make you into Americans." When they replied that they would rather be Lakota, we slaughtered them. Some people just cannot learn what it means to be free.

Christians, as honorary members of the Tribe of Israel, ought to have no quarrel with being called "tribalistic." The question is not, "Will you be a member of a tribe?" but rather, "Will the tribe that demands your allegiance be true or false?" "Will you be willing to share the Lord's table with the Pawnee?"

If tribalism is used in a negative sense, then nothing is more "tribal" than that which is called the United States of America. In the name of being a universal society, that tribe puts boundaries between peoples and defends them with murderous intensity. Tribalism resides wherever people are killed, no longer to preserve the divine right of kings, but rather to preserve "national sovereignty" and "territorial integrity" or "national self-determination."

A primary way in which the United States, through its Constitution, has sought to disarm troublesome Christians is by declaring that politics is public and that religion is private. Thus "religion" is allowed to preoccupy itself with "sexual issues" because sex also is "private." We are free to be as religious as we want, so long as we keep it to ourselves, so long as religion concerns itself with our innermost feelings and our deepest desires. This is an unsatisfactory account of a religion like Christianity, which believes that God, not nations, rules the world—a very public, political belief, indeed. But it also is a cynical device to make sure that Christians never fundamentally challenge the lordship of the state over our lives.

When United Methodist leader Jean Audrey Powers tells the world that she is a lesbian, this seems to us the beginning of an interesting public conversation about who should and who should not be a United Methodist pastor. What are the theological reasons why sexual orientation is an important clerical qualification? We believe that our church's thinking on this subject is muddled. Here is a woman who has served in a national position of the denomination for a number of years, revealing that her sexual orientation is at odds with what the church says that it requires from its pastors. She compares herself to the Hebrew slaves in Egypt and the United Methodist Church to Pharaoh.

Yet when Ms. Powers says that her sexual practices are nobody else's business, a private matter between her and her lover, she displays a dismayingly conventional, bourgeois notion of sexual practices. In our culture, sex is Pharaoh, that which rules our lives, or, more accurately, sex is one of the means whereby Pharaoh keeps us in bondage.

When issues of sexuality become matters of privacy, of choice, then you know that the battle is lost. "Choice makes it appear that questions of the disciplines associated with our lives have to do with our personal fulfillment and other corrupt bourgeois notions of sexuality. One of the reasons why the church asks us to be faithful sexually is because that is part of the discipline necessary to be a people capable of confronting the powers that would destroy our lives. For us, fidelity in marriage is a discipline necessary to sustain us in the struggle with the enemy.

Consider the discipline necessary for revolutionaries who would overthrow an established regime. They have no time for those who think that sexual pleasure is good in and of itself, that caring for their sexuality is more important than the revolution. Sex, like everything else, must be subjected to the discipline necessary to be the kind of people capable of fighting a war against injustice. The deepest problem of Christian ethics is that Christian practices like fidelity have lost their purpose as part of the formation of a community capable of sustaining itself in a world that constantly threatens to undermine it. The reason why Christians are called to be faithful in our marriages and prior to our marriages is because such faithfulness is intrinsic to a church at war.

Practices like fidelity are disciplines necessary for a people who know that the battle is long. Our struggle with the world is not going to be a one-night stand. Rather, the church is in a longtime struggle that requires people who have the virtues to sustain a long struggle. Faithfulness and the willingness to have children are the church's way of sustaining our lives in a world that is the enemy of long-term commitment to anyone, and especially to children.

For example, it is our belief that nothing is a more faithful witness to God's good care of God's people than the Jewish insistence on having children in the face of Christian persecution over the ages. The Jews refused to be tempted by the persecuting Christians to refrain from having children. That they were able to continue to have children in a world that was not safe is but an indication that they are God's promised people.

Indeed, we sometimes think that God has called Christians in the world so that Jews might be forced to live the way Jesus called us to live—that is, as a people who have sustained the skills over the centuries to survive as a people without an army. Jews had something better than an army. They had their worship and the habits of life that came from their worship to sustain them in a hostile world. This, we believe, is the great challenge for the church today. We must recover those habits that are still present among us but often only as memories that will sustain us in the fight.

Of course, this way of thinking about the church does require a rethinking of how questions are posed. For example, the suggestion that we are asking the church to withdraw from the world is based upon the presumption that the church must relate to its "culture." So we are told we must deal with the perennial question of the relationship between Christ and culture. The problem with putting the issue that way is that it presumes that the church, and the Christ we worship, is not itself a culture. The problem before us today is not how the church will serve its culture. We are already servile to this culture in too many ways!

The question is, How can the church be enculturated as a people capable of surviving in a culture that tempts us to forget that we ourselves, as the church, are a culture? How can our culture be an alternative to the cultures in which we find ourselves? Of course, there may be continuities between the culture that is the church and the culture in which we find ourselves. Cultural continuity, however, cannot be guaranteed, or desired, for much depends on how open a surrounding culture is to those who worship God. This continuity is something that the church discovers because it first knows who it is.

> *Now large crowds were traveling with him; and he turned and said to them, "Whoever comes to me and does not hate father and mother, wife and children, brothers and sisters, yes, and even life itself, cannot be my disciple. Whoever does not carry the cross and follow me cannot be my disciple. . . . What king, going out to wage war against another king, will not sit down first and consider whether he is able with ten thousand to oppose the one who comes against him with twenty thousand? If he cannot, then, while the other is still far away, he sends a delegation and asks for the terms of peace. So therefore, none of you can become my disciple if you do not give up all your possessions."*
> —Luke 14:25-27, 31-33

We recognize that part of the difficulty in coming to terms with resident aliens is that there seems to be such a distance between the churches that exist and the church we are calling into existence. People think that we are asking the church to be the Amish of Pennsylvania.

While we have great respect for the Amish of Pennsylvania, that is not who we are asking the church to be. We are after all mainstream Methodists. We believe that God has not abandoned even mainstream Methodists, as we possess habits—if we had the courage to draw upon them—that would provide exactly the kind of inculturation in the church we think necessary to sustain us in the fight.

For example, Stanley remembers a talk he heard long ago by an official of the World Council of Churches concerning the Orthodox response to the Communist party takeover in Russia. Few churches had more accommodated themselves to their social roles than had Russian Orthodoxy. One would have thought that the whole task of the Orthodox Church of Russia was to underwrite the rule of the czars. Obviously, its social reality was more complex than that, but there can be no question that the Russian Orthodox Church, at least in its official positions, was deeply accommodated to the rule of the czars. Its alleged "mystical worship" meant that there was very little sense of social engagement of the church in matters having to do with politics and economics. So when the Communists took power, here was a church peculiarly ill suited to resist the powers that be.

There was one Russian Orthodox habit, however, that brought the church out of the church. Before the

Eucharist, the priest was expected to go to the porch of the church and ring a handbell. The bell was to indicate to the people in the village that the celebration was beginning. The early Communist regime, however, as part of its anti-religious campaign, outlawed the traditional public ringing of the bell. Finally, the world had impinged on the church, and through that impingement the Orthodox discovered that the God they worshiped was indeed the God of the world. Orthodox priests, unfailingly traditionalist by nature, doggedly continued to stand on the porch, ringing their little bells, finding church impossible without the ringing of the bell. The state reacted by slaughtering and jailing priests by the thousands. Refusing to give up the ringing of the bell, Orthodoxy confronted its nation's rulers with a determination that they did not know they had. God, in God's mysterious ways, had made the Orthodox more faithful than they had ever wanted to be. Thank God for the Communists who figured out a way to make the church the Church.

In a similar fashion, we believe God is helping us discover the significance of the everyday practices of the church that are necessary to help us in the fight. For example, consider the fact that the church still requires people to be gathered in order to worship God. We are called out of our homes, out of our neighborhoods, out of our cities, to be gathered together as a people capable of worshiping God. That we do not worship God in our homes is a sign that we understand that the family can be as destructive as it can be sustaining. The church calls the family into question exactly to the extent that the church insists on educating our children that their loyalty to God is primary even to their loyalty to their family. We insist on telling our people that, as a gathered people on Sunday, the unity of the church is more determinative than the unity that the nation supplies.

Again, such a practice is the simple act of learning to pray to God. Learning to pray is the way Christians discover how to speak. The primary language of the church is the language of prayer—because in prayer the practice and the language are inseparable. Of course, it is not easy to learn to pray well. And that is why we do well to imitate those who have prayed before us. So we say prayers whose words we may not even well understand because in the saying we discover that we have become part of an understanding we can only later make our own. So by becoming skilled speakers of that language called Christian, through prayer we discover the skills necessary for Christians not only to survive but also to resist the world that would destroy us.

Accordingly, Christians cannot easily go to war against other nations in which we might be asked to kill Christians. How can we get up from the table of unity and be willing to kill one another in the name of loyalties that are not loyalties to Christ? What would it mean to rise from the table of unity we call Eucharist and kill one another in the name of national loyalties? Is it any wonder that the world does not take Christians seriously when we do so—because the world knows in effect we are the world's not God's.

A Christian's fight against war in many ways is too easy a target. Everyone is against war, but often Christians are against war for the wrong reasons. We have been taught to think that war is so terrible no Christian could be for it. The deep difficulty with war for the Christian is not that it is so terrible but that it destroys the unity of the Body of Christ. Indeed, part of being resident aliens is helping Christians to challenge the sentimentalities of liberal democratic polities, which presume that war must be some kind of misunderstanding that got out of control. War is the enemy of Christians because war urges us to sacrifice our children to the wrong gods, because it brings people together around the wrong symbols, because it deceives us into thinking that nations, not God, rule the world. War is incredible moral competition to the gospel. War brings out the best in people—there are few good novels and no good movies about peace. War requires incredible sacrifice. War draws a people together as they stand against a common foe. It is exactly because we understand what a high moral project war involves that we think the church must be the kind of people with the habits that enable them to challenge that moral project. So if you want to know where and how resident ali-

> *Be strong in the Lord and in the strength of his power. Put on the whole armor of God, so that you may be able to stand against the wiles of the devil. For our struggle is not against enemies of blood and flesh, but against the rulers, against the authorities, against the cosmic powers of this present darkness. . . . Therefore take up the whole armor of God, so that you may be able to withstand on that evil day, and having done everything, to stand firm. Stand therefore, and fasten the belt of truth around your waist, and put on the breastplate of righteousness . . . take the shield of faith. . . . Take the helmet of salvation, and the sword of the Spirit, which is the word of God.*
> —Ephesians 6:10-17

ens live, explore the development of those practices, those disciplines that might enable us to be the sort of people who have the resources to say, No, even to so great a moral project as war.

In the early Middle Ages, the great Burgundian monastery of Cluny launched an experiment with its feudal neighbors—landowners around the monastery who were always warring with one another. The arrangement, known as the "truce of God," was that all hostilities should be restricted to three days in the week (Monday to Wednesday). The experiment did not last long and, in retrospect, it may appear a bit silly. But it is more than a comical bit of medieval eccentricity. Behind it lay the honest insight that for baptized Christians, sharers in the Body of Christ, to be in a state of war with one another was ridiculous.[3] We believe that the Burgundians, with their great respect for the power of the symbolic, were on to something. After all, three days a week without war may not be everything, but one has to start somewhere.

Stanley has a poster on his office door that is sponsored by the Mennonite Central Committee. The poster reads: "A Modest Proposal for Peace—let the Christians of the world agree that they will not kill each other." Some might think that an insufficient gesture, somewhat akin to the Burgundian plan for three days a week without war. But what could be more radical than a Christian's unwillingness to kill other Christians because we understand that as a gathered people we are bound in a deeper unity than that which comes through family, neighborhood, or nation?

Imagine, in the international war against Iraq, if some Episcopalian, having seen Bishop Edmund

Browning celebrating the Eucharist at the Anglican church in Baghdad, had said, "I will do my duty for George Bush and Exxon in fighting Iraq, but I will not do anything that might endanger the lives of my fellow Anglicans in Baghdad." That you cannot even conceive of such a person is an indictment upon the church we have created, and one of the reasons why we need resident aliens.

At the end of John's gospel, in John 20, the Risen Christ appears to his disciples. Thomas, having missed the appearance, tells the others that he will not believe in the resurrection unless he touches the very wounds of the Risen Christ. When Christ urges Thomas to be "not faithless but believing," Thomas cries out, "My Lord and my God!"

Raymond Brown notes that Thomas's confession may be used by John, not only to express belief in the resurrection but also to make a political claim. *Dominus et Deus noster* was the title the emperor Domitian commanded every resident of the Empire to honor.[4] "Lord and Our God" was the royal ascription in use about the time John was written. With brilliant irony John has transformed a phrase associated with the imperial worship of power and glory, through Thomas's confession, to the Risen, crucified Christ. The one who still bears the scars of ignominy—the worst the Emperor could do to a rival— is the one who is now hailed by his church as our Lord and our God.

Think of Easter as a political rally. Think of Sunday worship, our handling of the broken body and the shed blood, as our attempt to get our politics right.

CHAPTER THREE

Church and World

The First Task of the Church

Our perspective on resident aliens can only be described as eschatological, if not apocalyptic. By eschatological yearnings, we Christians believe that we live in a world storied by God. It is a world with an end, and because it is a world with an end, it is also a world with a beginning. But the world cannot know that it is a world with an end and a beginning—without the church. There is not even a world unless there is a church.

As Karl Barth put it:

> The only advantage of the Church over against the world is that the Church knows the real situation of the world. Christians know what non-Christians do not. . . . It belongs to the Church to witness to the Dominion of Christ clearly, explicitly, and consciously.[1]

Stanley's repeated assertion that the first task of the church is not to make the world more just but to make the world the world is an eschatological claim. The very notion that you could write a history of the world is a notion that can only come from the presumption that a body of people exists called church who know the world better than the world can know itself. After all, without the church being a people who are universally connected across the nations, how else would the world know it is the world?

This, of course, makes much difference for how Christians are educated. We believe that nothing is more destructive for Christians in North America than the habits of mind we are taught in public schools. The narratives we are taught in those schools obscure the church as the teller of the tale of what it means for us to know the world as world. For example, when something called "history" is taught in a way that the church is but one character among the nations, then Christians lose the habits of mind necessary to understand the world from a Christian perspective. When history is taught as the history of nations, it is assumed that nations determine the destiny of the world, not God in God's care of God's world through the church.

In seminaries we teach a course called "American Church History." The very designation "American Church History" presumes

In those days a decree went out from Emperor Augustus that all the world should be registered. This was the first registration and was taken while Quirinius was governor of Syria. All went to their own towns to be registered. Joseph also went from the town of Nazareth in Galilee to Judea, to the city of David called Bethlehem, because he was descended from the house and family of David. He went to be registered with Mary, to whom he was engaged and who was expecting a child. While they were there, the time came for her to deliver her child. And she gave birth to her firstborn son and wrapped him in bands of cloth, and laid him in a manger, because there was no place for them in the inn.

—Luke 2:1-7

that the primary subject is America and the church's role in America. We think we should rather be teaching courses such as "The Church's Story of America." For example, it would be fascinating to tell that story from the perspective of what it means to be Christian in Zimbabwe—for the Christians in Zimbabwe are much more our brothers and sisters than our non-Christian brothers and sisters who happen to be American. Related to the claim that the first task of the church is to be the church is the recovery of habits of mind that give us the skills to understand the world in which we live on our terms and not on the world's terms.

At the beginning of Luke 2, we read history, at least history as it is taught in the schools. History is the story of men, powerful men like Emperor Augustus, the great Caesar who brought peace to all of the world during his reign. And if we have a special interest in classical studies, we may read even of Quirinius. These men, these mighty men who commanded armies, enacted laws, and ruled the world are men who make history, who determine the plot of the story of the world and, in Augustus's case, brought peace with justice to Judea.

But who are this Mary and Joseph inserted into history? Who is the *God* who inserts himself into history through Mary and Joseph? Luke skillfully begins his story of Jesus with conventional, official "history." But by the time the story ends, in just a few short verses, Luke has rearranged our idea of history. Where are Augustus and Quirinius now? These men, these mighty men, so significant in their own day, who, with the stroke of a pen could send these Jews packing across Judea to be registered, where are they now? Why must

Mary and Joseph be registered? They had to register for the same reason why black folk in South Africa had to carry identity cards under the rule of apartheid. Augustus can't keep up with these Jews without registration. And we realize why all the world was at peace. It was peace, *Pax Romana*, a Roman enforced peace with all the world under the heel of a ruthless dictator.

Where is Augustus now? Where is Quirinius? They are dead. By the time this story was being told by Luke they are rotting in their tombs somewhere. But that baby, wrapped in rags, lying in a manger, that baby for whom there was no room in the inn, that baby's people are dismantling the world of Augustus and Quirinius stone by stone.

Luke is tutoring us not to be too impressed by what the world calls "history." Be not taken in by what the world calls "news," for there is a good news beyond the news, outside conventional headlines.

The fundamentalists are right: What Christians get in public schools is destructive of the Christian faith. It is not destructive of the Christian faith, however, because science in and of itself undermines the presuppositions of creation, though often the way science is taught as a mechanistic system does challenge some of the basic presuppositions of the Christian faith. Rather, the deep problem for Christians in public education is that it's not "public education." It is nationalistic education. Horace Greeley, the foundational theorist for public education, was quite clear that the purpose of compulsory, state administered education was to integrate the swarming masses of immigrants into America.

Recently, in a radio interview, a Native American activist was asked, "What would you like this country to do for you and your people?"

"Well," he answered in a quiet, unemotional voice, "one small thing the government could do for us is to return Mount Rushmore to the state in which they found it."

"What?" asked the astounded interviewer.

"It would be a start, a small thing, but a start. You can imagine how humiliating it is for us to have had one of our sacred mountains defaced with the images of some of the bloodiest leaders in history—Roosevelt, Washington, Jefferson, and a man like Lincoln. It's bad for our children to look up and see those images carved into stone. Some of them might take them as examples they ought to follow. What if some of our children grew up to be like Jefferson?"

We daresay that here was someone who had escaped the indoctrination of the public schools. Here was someone working out of a very different story about the way the world is.

When George Bush said, "We must oppose naked aggression wherever it occurs around the world," Christians had been so indoctrinated by public education that we thought that we were included in that "we." Resident aliens are discovering that what it means to be church is quite different from what it means to tell a story that makes a better world. Think of Sunday morning worship as a clash of narratives. In other words, the one who gets to tell the story is the one who determines the politics.

Resident aliens have a different conception of "politics" than that which currently captures the imagination of the church. Christians, by nature of our faith, are very "political." It's just that we have a more interesting view of what being "political" means. As we said in *Resident Aliens*, when the world asks us, "Say something political," we say, "Church."

There is some evidence, based upon our story, that the primary biblical way of dealing with politics is as a joke. In one of the few places in the Old Testament where laughter is mentioned, it is the laughter of God over the state of the united nations: "He who sits in the heavens laughs; the LORD has them in derision" (Psalm 2:4). Later in the same psalm, when the psalmist advises kings on what they should do to handle so great a king as Yahweh, he tells the kings to "kiss his feet" (although the exact translation of the euphemism is uncertain, for the psalmist may be telling kings to kiss another part of the divine anatomy).

When politics is brought to the attention of Jesus (Luke 20:20-26), the whole discussion is portrayed with such jocularity as to suggest that we are to take none of this with seriousness. When wanting to trap Jesus and hand him over to the police (Luke 20:20), they ask Jesus, "Should we pay taxes to Caesar or not?" (Note that this was *our* question, not Jesus'.)

Jesus answers (Luke 20:24), "Who's got a quarter?" (Note that Jesus' pockets are empty.)

When a coin is produced, Jesus asks, "Whose picture is on it?"

We answer, "George Washington."

"Well, if he needs the stuff so badly as to put his picture on it, then give it to him," says Jesus. "But you be careful and don't give to Caesar what belongs to God."

Okay. We give up. Should we pay taxes to Caesar or not?

From this we learn that a primary biblical way of treating politics is as a joke. Certainly, politicians can make much mischief, but it would be a liturgical and ethical mistake to take them too seriously. Idolatry is as big a problem for democracies as for non-democracies.

Continuing the political fun into the book of Acts, we find an assortment of pagan bureaucrats and functionaries parading through, none of whom is pictured with much sympathy by Luke. Felix, Agrippa, Bernice, and all the rest are the beneficiaries of some of the most eloquent apostolic testimony, and absolutely none of them ever gets the point. Acts depicts a church busily interfacing with the world, always probing, always on the move, always willing to talk to anyone—even a pagan Roman bureaucrat—who will listen. However, the results of such political witness and public hearings are slim. About the best one can expect from such political action, according to the Acts of the Apostles, is the liberal, open-minded, pagan sigh: "Well, this dialogue is *awfully* interesting. We'll just have to hear more about this sometime." But never conversion. And in the end, the politicians react to the church in the typical Gentile way—Paul is executed in Rome.

From these stories in Acts we derive a number of principles for Christian engagement with politics:

1. We must never give Caesar more than his due. Never take Caesar or his solutions with too much seriousness.
2. Christians are in the world; therefore, we run various skirmishes into the political world. We are

every bit as "public" and "political" as anyone, even more so.

3. However, do not expect much from politics. Invariably, politicians tend to be totalitarian—be they the democratically elected type or the socialist collectivist type—because bureaucrats are bureaucrats. That is, most bureaucrats, down deep, act as if there were no God. They have an infinite means of co-opting and corrupting the gospel. Be careful around managers. A bureaucrat's self-interest is larger than yours.

4. In the end, no matter how congenial the conversation, no matter how many concessions we win from politics, the bottom line for the way the world congregates and unifies people is violence. Politics and violence go together. Violence tends to be the predominant means for establishing community in a world that knows not a God who calls a family named church.

Perhaps this is what Fuller Seminary's Miroslav Volf means when he speaks of the Christian difference with the world being a "soft difference." Volf says that a "soft" difference does not mean "weak."[2] We really do have fundamental differences with the way the world orders itself. However, our difference is not a difference that is open to threats or coercion. Our difference does not mean that we think that the world is more evil than we, that we think that we are redeemed and the world is fallen. We believe that the world and the church are both fallen *and* redeemed by the cross of Christ. It's just that the church knows this and is attempting to live in the light of that knowledge, whereas the world does not know this. Perhaps the world's lack of knowledge is the fault of the church, rather than the error of the world. How vibrant, engaging, and enticing has been the witness of the church to the world? Jesus has clearly entrusted the salvation of the world to the church rather than to the world.

"The soft difference is the missionary side of following in the footsteps of the crucified Messiah. It is not an optional extra but part of Christian identity itself," says Volf.[3] In being missionaries in the world of politics, we realize that we are in a particularly dangerous location, considering the political history of this century, a place that, time and again, has perverted and co-opted the Christian faith for its ungodly purposes. Yet "politics" is not a monolithic place, and "politics" is also meant to come under the Lordship of Christ. And he will rule until he has brought all things under his feet (Hebrews 2:8), the same feet that all kings are commanded to kiss (Psalm 2:4).

Will never tires of telling about the Sunday a few years ago when he was visiting a congregation where, during the Sunday service, the preacher indulged in a practice not dear to our hearts—a "Children's Sermon." The boys and girls were called down front. Squatting in the chancel.

The preacher began, "Boys and girls, today is Epiphany. Can you say, 'Epiphany'? Epiphany falls on January 6, and, today it falls on Sunday. Isn't that great boys and girls? Epiphany means *revelation, manifestation.* A favorite Epiphany story is found at the beginning of Matthew's Gospel. You know the story. It's the story of the wise men who came to Bethlehem to see the baby Jesus. But they weren't really 'Wise Men' or even

'Three Kings.' The Bible calls them Magi. *Magi.* That's where we get our word *magic.* They were magicians, or astrologers (the kind Mrs. Reagan uses). [No laughter in congregation.] They came 'from the East.' Some people think they came from Persia. Boys and girls, where is Persia? [Silence. One child ventures, 'Iran?']

"Yes, Iran. Good. That was Persia, but it wasn't all of Persia. What other countries are located in what was Persia?"

One child says, "Iraq?"

"Iraq! Good! Iraq. In fact, some people think that these Magi came from Baghdad, capital of Iraq. There were lots of these Magi in Iraq. . . . And Matthew says these Magi, these Iraqis, were the first to get an Epiphany, the first to see and to worship the baby Jesus. A lot of people who had the Bible, a lot of people who thought they were close to God missed it, and these strange people from Iraq saw it."

Now what would be the effect of telling a story like that, of teaching history like that to a group of North American children? We expect that many of them would walk out of church seeing the world a bit differently, realizing a definite disjuncture between church and world on the basis of our story.

Church-World

The fundamental theological notion that is informing H. Richard Niebuhr's *Christ and Culture* is the relationship between creation and redemption. "Churches" have creation as their main interest, in great part because creation has been so good to them. "Sects" have redemption as their focus, mainly because creation has been so bad to them that they feel a stronger need for redemption. That is, theologically it is assumed that creation and redemption are primary theological descriptions that should determine how one understands what is going on in the world.

I suspect that Hauerwas is most liked by those whose religious traditions have always been suspicious of classical, systematic theologies, high culture and abstract thinking, and who feel the sting when the pieties of their youth are treated with disdain in the universities. Some people do not want to be forced to give an account of the faith that is within them, or do not know how to, or think that it is improper even to ask for such an account. They like Hauerwas's convenient philosophic conviction that since all claims are equally without foundation, religious claims are immune to rational criticism. They want theos without logos.[4]
—Max Stackhouse

In contrast, we assume the relationship between *church-world* is more primary than the described distinction between creation and redemption.

This is part of our theory for why many Presbyterians do not like *Resident Aliens*. Not only has Niebuhr's *Christ and Culture* found its most congenial home among many of them—they enjoy thinking of themselves as socially significant transformers of American culture—but also they think (contra Calvin) that a theology of creation can be abstracted from redemption. They think that it is possible to devise independent criteria about nature that are separate from Christology. This leads them to praise "creation" in a way that not only sentimentalizes the environment, thus making our ecological destruction incomprehensible, but also implies that the world does not need redemption. We claim that we really have no way of knowing what the world is, where it is headed, or what it needs from us before meeting this Jew from Nazareth named Jesus.

In his wonderful book *Believing Three Ways in One God*, Nicholas Lash notes that the spring festival, rather than mid-winter, once marked New Year's Day. On March 25, according to one fifth-century calendar known as the Martyrology of Jerome, this was said: "Our Lord Jesus Christ was crucified, and conceived, and the world was made."[5] That world is God's creation in which all things were brought out of nothing. By God's word God made a home in the world, in a virgin's womb. That is the history we Christians must learn, to tell about what it means for our God to be creator.

The church is the carrier of the memory of creation in Mary so that the world may know where it began. That is the reason why, we suspect, much to our surprise, many Episcopalians are warmed by the idea of resident aliens. They are one of the few church families in the North American context who stress ecclesiology and can therefore see that Christian theology begins in ecclesiology, in church practices, not in something called "Systematic Theology." Theology begins in church and works its way out, rather than beginning in a university department of religion and dribbling back to the church as the practical application of great thoughts.

Most seminary curricula embody this mistake. For example, we teach systematic theology as something that is necessary to do prior to teaching ethics. This presupposes that you have to get your ideas systematized before you talk about practices. As a result, we fail to see that theology itself is a practice in service to the church, which is in service to the world. Resident aliens challenge the presumption that theology is about ideas. Our presupposition that church, then world, is the primary category is meant to remind us that practices are more important than ideas. Indeed, the very creation of the notion of "idea" suggests that the church has already lost its moorings from the habits that sustain it. We want to help Christians discover modes of how the church can be enculturated as the church.

Again, it is important to remember that no practice more determines the church's being than how we have learned to speak the church's language.

One of the great tasks before the church today is to teach one another how to speak. When we say "world," it is not the same thing that *The New York Times* means when it says "world." This ambiguity about the term *world* can be a deeply confusing matter for Christians. And that is why it *is* so important that we be possessed by habits and practices that help us remember that our language works quite differently than the world's language.

Unfortunately, to an embarrassing degree, our inability to know how to speak well is a result of the disciplinary divisions currently characteristic of mainstream Protestant seminaries. For example, the way we separate Old Testament from New Testament, systematic theology from ethics, or preaching from biblical studies becomes complicitous as a mode of making sure that the church does not take itself seriously in relationship to its mission to make the world more obviously "the world."

So the church serves the world by helping the world know that it is the world. The world is all of that which has used God's patience not to worship God. That it does so leaves the world in deep distress. The church therefore serves the world exactly to the extent such distress can be named. You do not know how to cure a disease until you can name it. That is what resident aliens are urging. Our first task as Christians today, if we are to serve well in the world in which we find ourselves, is to name the illness.

The first task of the church (to make the world the world rather than to make the world more just) becomes more intelligible once we understand that morally you can only act in the world that you can see, and you can only see by learning to say. In other words, our understanding of what it means to be Christian is to submit ourselves to the discipline of learning how to speak a foreign language. The church's language is not a natural language, but it is a language that requires the self to be transformed to be part of that language. Our colleague at Duke, Alasdair MacIntyre, has convinced us, in *Whose Justice, Which Rationality?* that languages are languages in use. Language is a set of practices rather than a collection of words.

That is why translation of Christian practices or terms (such as *eucharist* and *sin*) into more relevant and acceptable ideas is always such a doubtful business. To make their beliefs more palatable, some church leaders think that they can translate peculiar Christian terms into concepts that will attract worldly unbelievers through the door. These people are called "seekers." In fact, they are hoping to attract people in the world who are just like them, for the resulting difference between church and world is too often imperceptible. To upset sensitive church managers who are looking for other nice people to share their church facilities, Stanley always tells people that they can't understand his use of the word *asshole*. If Stanley calls Will "asshole," people think that Stanley is making a negative judgment about Will. But where Stanley comes from (Texas), this is a term of endearment. To know that, one needs to be part of the practices of Texas where males are allowed to touch one another only after they've scored a touchdown. "Asshole" becomes one of the ways of saying, "I'm certainly glad you're my friend because we share the same practices."

American Christians, living under the erroneous assumption that this is at least a vestigially Christian nation, fail to appreciate the oddness of our language. We act as if anyone, regardless of skills, insights, and training, ought to be able to walk in off the street and understand what we are saying. Just as you can't learn French by reading a French novel in an English translation, so also you can't learn the gospel by hearing it translated through the language of self-esteem (I'm okay, you're okay) or the marketing jargon (God is your CEO) of American capitalism.

When we say *child* the world may think that it understands what we mean by that word. However, the world does not know the stories that make that word intelligible, stories of a Savior who embraced children, blessed children, who said, "Whenever you receive one of these little ones in my name, you receive me." About all the world can do with the word *child* is to sentimentalize it or else dispose of it, because in a world were people are valued on the basis of their achievements and products, children are always under threat.

God came to us, says Luke, as a child. God made war on the Caesars, not through an army, but by a baby. Knowing that story forms the church, helps us for the first time to see the world.

An Invitation to Be Odd

Hauerwas and Willimon believe that the role of the church is to be the church, "the only community formed around the truth, which is Jesus Christ, who is the truth, the life and the way."... And they argue that the two main modes of modern Christian thought, the "conversionist" (typically conservative) and the "activist" (typically liberal) are both conformed to the world. For Hauerwas and Willimon, the church is not "liberal" or "conservative" in the world's terms, but a radical alternative to both, the community of the cross.

Because they define the church first and foremost as a confessing body determined to worship Jesus Christ in all things, these two southern-born-and-bred Methodists have found themselves accused of "sectarianism" and "tribalism." Will Willimon recalled such a conversation at the Episcopal Theological Seminary of the Southwest in Austin, Texas.

After a lecture, Willimon was admonished by a listener. "I sense a disturbing sectarian drift in your thought."

Willimon replied "Look, you're an Episcopalian in Texas. You've got your nerve calling me a sect. I would think that the average Episcopalian in the average little town in Texas feels like someone being a member of a sect group."

Reflecting on the exchange, Willimon went on, "And I'm saying, that's you (Episcopalians) at your best. I learned a lot from Episcopalians in South Carolina, in little southern towns. Their attitude is, we're Episcopalians and here's what we do. If you don't like it, that's okay. No hard feelings, but this is what we do. Episcopalians at their best have been a kind of countercultural influence."

Convinced as they are about the obligation of the church to be faithful in all things, Willimon and Hauerwas have no patience with the liberal "affirming" mode of pastoral care. As an example, they describe what typically happens when a young woman appears in the church office and tells the pastor she is pregnant and unable to handle her pregnancy alone.

"What would that woman do if we said, look, you know abortion is wrong, you should bear this child?" they ask. "The typical response would be wait a minute. I'm 19 years old, I can't have this baby by myself." And she's absolutely right, she can't. Which then would stick it to us—we good liberal pastors need to come clean with ourselves. A lot of these sensitive, affirming positions we're holding are simply this: the person we're looking after is ourselves. We have next to nothing to offer to that woman to help her have that baby. And people like her come back and remind us how little of a church we've got."[6]

—Bonnie Shullenberger

We think that nothing is more important than for the church to be a community capable of being obedient to authority. No issue more bedevils our lives today than the problem of the loss of authority. In America all claims to authority cannot help appearing authoritarian. This is the result of the presumption that democratic freedom means that we each get to be our own tyrants. This personal authority is but another name for hell, since there we are forced to do what previously we only wanted to do.

In few places is the boundary between the church and the world seen more clearly than in the issue of authority. We live in a world that assumes it has "solved" the "problem" of authority by making each person his or her own tyrant. But in the church we know we live under authority—under the word, under the authority of the bishop charged with reminding us how to live in unity with Christians across time and space.

The great difficulty with the ordained ministry today is that in our present context ministers too often think their authority depends upon being perpetually pleasant—and unfortunately we attract people to the ministry who have this gift. There's nothing in and of itself wrong with being perpetually pleasant, but often such people lack the courage necessary to act with authority in the church.

Stanley was recently confronted by one of his former students, a man who came from a brick-laying background like himself, who had been in the military and come late to the ministry. He is an extraordinarily serious man who served in a United Methodist conference in the South but refused to seek ordination as elder since he was not sure he had been appropriately examined.

He suddenly appeared in Stanley's office to tell him he had left United Methodism and had become Orthodox. He had seen a book in a Christian bookstore called *What Is Orthodoxy?* but resisted buying it, since it cost $8.50. However, he finally bought it and read it voraciously three times. He suddenly realized that he had found his home. So he moved to another city to associate with an Orthodox church through which he could be initiated into the patterns and practices of Orthodoxy and look forward to ordination as an Orthodox priest. Hauerwas observed that he was a long way from south Alabama.

On being questioned what ever could have led him to make such a move, he responded simply, "They don't vote on the truth."

Unfortunately in most American Protestant denominations, we have acted as if we could vote on the truth, on our mission, and on our practices. We did not understand that our task is to become a disciplined people capable of acknowledging the truth that has made us what we are through being led in worship by those who are worthy. Worthiness does not denote that the clergy knows more than the laity. But rather, the ordained ministry is embodied by those who have the courage and humility to remind the church of those practices necessary for us to be in unity with God, with one another, and with the church universal. We need people in the ministry who are able to say to those of us who are in the laity that of course we do not understand why we should act in this way, because we haven't done the work necessary for such understanding.

Note that such an account of authority is not blind. It does not assume that men have a better vision of the truth than do women. It is not the imposition of one arbitrary will on another arbitrary will. But rather obedience to such an authority denotes a relationship that comes from a history that helps us understand that our obedience is a form of service to one another. So authority and obedience are part of the practices necessary for the people of God to withstand a society that has no understanding of such authority. We Christians do not just obey to obey, but we obey because the God we worship has been faithful to us. Our God is no willful tyrant but rather the one who unfailingly discerns our desires rightly. Our God has given us the time to discover that if we are patient with one another through our worship, we can become one mighty prayer of unity for the world. So we often do that which we do not understand, and in the process we become God's church.

For example, Stanley was told by a former pastor that as part of Lent we were to fast every Wednesday. Fasting to Stanley always seemed to be an invitation to narcissism, since it only reminded him of his needs. But he did it because his pastor commanded him to do it. In the process, he discovered not only what it meant to be in unity with his brothers and sisters in the church but also what it meant to hunger for God. We must rediscover such simple disciplines if we are to be a people who have power to stand against the world for the world's salvation.

In particular we must be a people willing to call to the ministry those we believe to have the courage and the humility to act with authority. Such people may not be the brightest, but they must be the people who are willing to subject their lives to the disciplines necessary for being people able to act with authority. Without such people, the church will lose its way, forgetting the story that makes it possible to be a disciplined body of people against the false stories of the world. Without this kind of authority, we lose the habits necessary to be a church that can recognize the multiplicity of the goods represented in the lives of the people of the church. This cannot help being "out of sync" with the way the world is.

Of course, it may be a mistake to concentrate on the ministry, though we think it important, involved as we are in seminary education. After all, God continues to raise up people among us, many laity being more faithful than those in ministry. It is the church's ministry that makes it possible for some to be ordained to do for the church what only the whole church can do. Yet it would be equally false to act as if those who are called to the ministry are finally a matter of indifference. The truth of the matter is that the best and the brightest are not coming to seminary today. That should not be surprising, given the loss of the church's social power and status. Those of talent look elsewhere for success.

Yet we know that God has given us people of talent, and we as the church must call them into the ministry whether they want to or not. We must say, "You have the gifts, and we need you." That is a true call, since it's not a matter of whether you really "want" to be in the ministry. We believe that then we might have a ministry among us who are saved from being the kind of flatterers so characteristic of the contemporary Protestant ministry. We believe then we could have a people capable of sustaining conflict as part of their faithful service to God. Then the world could say, "My, what an extraordinary people. See how they love one another. Indeed, they love one another enough even to call one another to account."

CHAPTER FOUR

Practice Discipleship

Embodiment

Some critics have accused us of providing a theological rationale for adjustment to a sociological reality. That is, the American church has been disestablished, pushed to the perimeter, forced to sit on the sidelines as the world debates the great issues of the day. We come along and say something obvious to the church, "Fine. Let's hunker down and enjoy sitting on the bench as the real games of life are played by others. Let's be 'resident aliens.'"

The American church has suffered under sociological determinism for so long, it is difficult to get the church to believe that our theological convictions could possibly be as determinative of our lives as "sociological reality." Long ago Ernst Troeltsch convinced suspicious scholars that "the whole Christian world of thought and dogma" arises out of "the fundamental sociological conditions, on the idea of fellowship which was dominant at any given time."[1] The only theological debate, therefore, is therefore over what actually is our sociological reality. Once that is named, theology helps us to adjust to that reality.

The sociological environment shapes our theological convictions, said Troeltsch, say contemporary Marxist

theologians, feminist theologians, and right-wing advo-
cates of the theology of the American Way. So Troeltsch
thought that the disenfranchised sect, alienated from
the dominant culture, of necessity stressed the Christ
as commanding "Lord," while the more acculturated
and accommodated church was forced, by its sociological situation, to serve a gracious "Redeemer."

John Milbank has helped us see how the way we've
been taught to think by Troeltsch cannot help resulting
in the domestication of the gospel.[2] We are defined by
our context and the surrounding culture. Sociology, at
least the kind of sociology exemplified by Troeltsch and
many others who currently work in the sociology of
religion, is an attempt to make us believe that the way
things are is the way things have to be. The world sets
the agenda. The difficulty is how the church can claim
its own sociology in a way that narrates the church's life,
without that narration becoming a comforting proposal
for why we really do not have to be at war in the society
in which we find ourselves. Every ethic implies a sociology (says Alasdair MacIntyre), but the crucial issue is
what kind of sociology. We believe the sociological
reality of the church is to be a gathered people separated from the world so that the world may know it is
the world.

In contrast, most contemporary theological and biblical interpretations are based on functional accounts
of the sociology of the church. These explanations find
it virtually impossible to consider religious practices
other than in service to the dominant social order.
Accordingly, our church leaders find it hard to imagine
any valid theology other than that which is used to tell
us as Christians that our task is to make the world a

better place. The difficulty is that this better place is defined by the world, and in particular by that funny group of people whom we call sociologists.

Douglas Sloan tells the sad story of how the churches lost their colleges and universities. Sloan demonstrates how even "Christian thinkers," like the Niebuhrs and Tillich, while complaining about the inadequacy of scientific knowledge, played by the established rules of the university—the fact/value dichotomy, mechanistic views of science, the preference for quantitative over qualitative knowing, and the essentially naturalistic conception of knowledge. Far from offering a substantial challenge to the modern university's thinking, having accepted the university's rules for thought, these would-be intellectual defenders of the faith did little more than offer a thin Christian veneer to that knowledge, which the university had readily available from a host of socially approved sources. Sloan says:

> In the end the theologians pulled back from affirming unambiguously the real possibility of knowledge of God and of the spiritual world. They again and again resisted seeking or talking about knowledge of God for fear of the danger of applying objectifying and manipulative modes of thought where they did not belong. At the same time, however, they wanted to affirm fully and without question, lest they be thought religious fundamentalists, the same objective, analytic modes of modern science and historical analysis in every other domain besides faith. The result was a split that forced the theological reformers back onto faith presuppositions whenever they spoke about religion, and onto an increasing reliance on naturalistic approaches to the

sensible world whenever they wanted to speak about
ethics, science, or knowledge in general.[3]

As resident aliens we might say that the theologians'
failure was more "political" than, as Sloan says, intellectual. Having accepted the boundaries for investiga-
tion and discourse set by the dominant culture, their
thought ventured only as far as those boundaries would
allow. Failing to see the fundamental challenge offered
by the Christian faith to such commonplace words as
intellectual, thought, and *reason,* they gave up too
much ground before the war. As a result, their battle
was lost before it began. Now, as that "modern world"
to which they so desperately wanted to speak loses its
privileged position in Western thought, their theology
seems quaint and provincial. As is often said, those
thinkers who marry the spirit of this age are doomed to
be widowed by the next.

The pathos of our current predicament can be seen
by asking what a Christian university might look like.
The truth is, we have no idea. Universities that bear the
name today usually talk about taking care of the "whole
student." This usually results in trying to regulate students' lives in a manner that their parents would no
longer even pretend to try. What we have lost is any
sense that the Christian practices of the church should
produce a different kind of knowledge than is represented at Christian universities.

Such a suggestion, of course, produces the startled
question, "Does that mean you believe that there is a
Christian economics, a Christian sociology, a Christian
philosophy, a Christian physics?" The answer is quite
simply, *yes.* It is not enough for Christians to teach

those subjects, because, as George Marsden points out in his book *The Soul of the American University*, often such teaching is done from the perspective of methodological atheism.[4] They don't really need a Trinity to make their knowledge work. We need Christians who say what difference their knowledge makes for the way we practice our lives.

Take, for example, the separation that is assumed in the contemporary university between economics and politics. This separation is due to capitalist presumptions, which assume that economics is a "science." This science has its own laws and is subject to no theology beyond production and distribution of wealth itself. How could a "Christian economist" produce that distinction if we were living faithfully? We do not believe that our money can be separated from our politics, and accordingly the way we think about these matters and teach them in the university could reflect such practices. A church that could produce such knowledge, and therefore a university, could not help standing as an alternative to a capitalist social order.

Will wrote about resident aliens while teaching one summer in Germany. Now he realizes how much his location in a strange place had influenced his writing. (William Stringfellow was typing *An Ethic for Christians and Other Aliens in a Strange Land* when the FBI broke into his home and arrested Daniel Berrigan for his anti-government protest activity. Stringfellow always said that this location influenced his writing.) The German church stands as a great rebuke to the church of any age, reminding us of the perils of a church in service to the surrounding political order. Troeltsch himself was a product of this church, a church that found it impossible to conceive a purpose for the church other than the improvement of Germany and the advancement of *Kultur*.

Will remembers a conversation with his faculty hosts, who asked, "Herr Doktor Willimon, why are you so interested in German language and culture?"

He responded, "Because I'm from South Carolina, I of course feel such a kinship with the Germans."

"Kinship?" they asked uneasily.

"Yes. Like you, we got caught red handed, justifying a vast evil. Unlike you, American slavery was not quite as efficient as your Holocaust. Southerners have never been too well organized. Yet our churches do have much in common."

In our opinion, the contemporary German church continues down this disastrous path. Having convinced itself that its great sin in the 1930s was conservatism, or nationalism, the new German church decides to be always on the left in any political discussion, hoping that this will ensure that it will avoid the pitfalls of the 1930s and will help to create a more just Germany. It is the same project, now pursued on the left, that led to such vast infidelity earlier. Sociology names the battle and determines the limits of the church's imagination.

We admit to being sociological determinists, at least to a degree. We do believe that Troeltsch was right in pointing to the strength of the surrounding sociological order in shaping our belief. A Christian community is also a sociological order; its beliefs and practices arise out of a way of life together.

Thus we are uninterested in debates about "Christ and Culture"—in how much we should have of one or the other. We live in North America or anywhere else as a Christian community, as a culture. Arguments over disembodied Christian "belief" are not as interesting as debates over the specific sociological embodiments of the gospel within this or that surrounding pagan social order. In baptism, Christians are given a new citizenship, a new home which makes all the difference in how we live in relationship to present arrangements.

"But you are a chosen race, a royal priesthood, a holy nation, God's own people" (1 Peter 2:9).

Learning the Language, Getting the Moves

The closest analogy we have seen for our stress on practice comes from, of all places, the Marine training camp at Parris Island:

"New" Marines Illustrate Growing Gap Between Military and Society

Corps Instills 'Family Values' and Beavis Finds Himself Critical of Civilian Culture

Parris Island, SC—After just eight weeks at boot camp, Andrew Lee has come to love the Marines and despise civilians. "People outside military life are repulsive," says Recruit Lee, the top member of Platoon 3086, as he cleans his M-16 rifle. "I think America could use a lot more military discipline."

Parris Island routinely transforms the Beavises and Butt-Heads of America into United States Marines. After 11 weeks here, recruits emerge self-disciplined, with a serious bearing. They are drug free, physically fit, and courteous to their elders. They have overcome deep differences of class and race and learned to live and work as a team.

But they do all that by becoming members of a military service that is pervaded with disdain for the society it protects. Like Recruit Lee, many of the young men in Platoon 3086 will leave Parris Island with a patriotism at odds with much of American culture. At home on post-graduation leave, they will feel estranged from old friends and society at large.

Yawning Gap

Parris Island proclaims itself to be "Where the Difference Begins." There always has been some distance between the Marines and American society, but it has grown wider since the 1970s. Back then the U.S. Military hit what may have been its all-time low point. Driven by military defeat, racial tension, drug abuse and widespread insubordination, the Marines came close to being a broken family.

The military rebounded. Unlike American society, it confronted its race and drug problems in effective ways. While there were 1,096 violent racial incidents in the Marines in 1970, today a whiff of racism will end a career. Drug use also has been minimized by a policy of "zero tolerance. . . ."

These days, drill instructors say they are contending with the children of the 1970s, a passive generation raised by baby sitters and day-care centers and one unaccustomed to accountability. "The broken-family kids are one of the bigger problems we have," says First Sgt. Charles Tucker. "A lot of them, if they come from a single-parent household and their mothers work, have had pretty much free rein. . . ."

Marine basic training is more a matter of cultural indoctrination than of teaching soldiering, which comes later. Staff Sgt. Gregory Biehl, the receiving sergeant, says in a private moment, "The Corps is like a family, and we teach family values."

Over the next 11 weeks, the recruits will learn the Marine way of talking, walking, and thinking. Every waking moment will remind them they have left a culture of self-gratification and entered a culture of self-discipline. Here pleasure is suspect and sacrifice is good. The recruits will be denied all the basic diversions of the typical American youth —television, cigarettes, cars, candy, soft-drinks, video games, music, alcohol, drugs, and sex.

Sgt. Biehl immediately immerses them in the Marines' peculiarly nautical language, in which doors are "hatches" and hats "covers." The next step in stripping away their identities is a ban on using the first person. Coming from a society that elevates the individual, they are now in a world where the group is supreme—and in which "I" is banished. Later in the day, a bleary-eyed Jonathan Parish, the self-declared Mobile skinhead, will try seven times before formulating a simple request in proper Marine style: "Sir, Recruit Parish requests permission to make a head call, sir."

The sun rises on a group shorn of its past. "Everything is taken away—hair, clothes, food and friends," says Navy Lt. James Osendorf, a Catholic chaplain here. "It's a total cutoff from previous life. . . . "

The sergeants use rest periods between drill practice to teach basic Marine "knowledge." There is nothing elegant about this: 19th century rote methods, usually shouted at full blast.

"Knowledge is what?" begins Sgt. Carey.

"Power, sir," responds the platoon, squatting on the cement.

"And power is what?"

This puzzles the platoon. "Money?" ventures one recruit.

"I swear, I'm dealing with aliens," says Sgt. Carey, dumbfounded by that civilian attitude persisting in his platoon after three days on the island. "No!" he shouts. "Power is victory!"

Unlike many in American society, Sgt. Carey and his fellow drill instructors aren't in it for the money. He works as long as 17 hours a day, 6 1/2 days a week. He is paid $1,775 a month—a figure that works out to be about the minimum wage.

Training

Several recruits in 3086 crumble in the first three weeks, a difficult phase when they are cut off from their old lives but don't yet feel like Marines. About 11% of all Marine recruits wash out during boot camp. . . .

The next day, Sgt. Carey preparing the platoon for its first major inspection, pulls a hanging thread from the starched camouflage uniform of Tony Wells. "You accept substandard performance," he shouts. "That's why America will fall one day, just like the Roman Empire fell. But not me, understand? But not me!"

But they are changing. Recruit Manczka is rewarded for high marksmanship by being allowed to call home to Edinboro, Pa.

"Hi, Mom," he says in a voice hoarsened from shouting responses to orders 17 hours a day.

"Who is this?" she asks. . . . .

Warrior Week

By Week 8, when the recruits march into the piney woods for infantry training, they are more Marine than civilian. All the "overweights" have reached their weight goals. The platoon is tanned, muscular and a bit cocky. Ordered to jump off a 47 foot high repelling platform, they do so with ease.

They no longer think about quitting. As they march along a causeway, the platoon mocks its dropouts with its own "casualty cadence":

"Hope you like the sights you see/Parris Island casualty.

As for you, it's still a dream/ On May 19 we are Marines."

They are growing comfortable with the Marines' culture of controlled violence. "An M-16 can blow someone's head off at 500 meters." Sgt. Paul Norman relates. "That's beautiful, isn't it?"

"Yes, sir," shout the 173 voices. . . .

"Being a Marine," he muses, "is the greatest thing in the world."

At 9 p.m. as the lights are switched off, the recruits lie in bed at attention for the "Protestant prayer." ("Lord God, help us to become United States Marines . . .") and a nearly identical "Catholic prayer. . . ."

Civilian society now seems remote to the platoon. . . . Eric Didler, who came here from the posh Washington suburb of Potomac, MD, criticizes civilian life as "lazy and unstructured." Another four recruits call it "nasty. . . ."

The black and Hispanic recruits, about one-fourth of the platoon, also think a bit of Parris Island would ease racial tensions "because Marine Corps discipline is also about brotherhood. . . ."

Depot Sgt. Maj. James Moore, the top sergeant on Parris Island, has monitored the attitudes of recruits since 1969. He thinks re-entry into society is more difficult than ever. "When I came up, I think there was more teaching of patriotism," says Sgt. Major Moore. "We prayed in school. In the Marines, we still put an emphasis on patriotism, on being unselfish, on trying to serve society." These days, he adds, far too many recruits come in with little moral foundation. "It is a fact of life," he adds, "that there isn't a lot of teaching in society about the importance of honor, courage, and commitment. It's difficult to go back into a society of 'what's in it for me?' "[5]

—Wall Street Journal

Note what the Marines did to their new recruits: They put them in a group, they moved them through a perilous ordeal, they taught them a new language, they gave them skills to analyze what was wrong with their former lives. Note that the world is also getting nervous that these young Marines, having experienced a new world, may be a threat to the old. Note that the closest

As many of you as were baptized into Christ have clothed yourselves with Christ. There is no longer Jew or Greek, there is no longer slave or free, there is no longer male and female; for all of you are one in Christ Jesus. And if you belong to Christ, then you are Abraham's offspring, heirs according to the promise.

—Galatians 3:27-29

Christian analogy we can think of for Marine basic training is the church's historic process of Christian initiation, that is, *baptism.*

In baptism, the church inculcates in us a set of practices whereby we become disciples. One of the challenges for new Christians is learning the language of this faith. There are so many odd words. Learning the language of Christianity is itself a practice. That is what Stanley means, for example, when he says that sin is not natural but rather we must be taught by the church to be a sinner. To be able to confess one's sin is a theological achievement, for sin is not some generalized assumption that we all do something wrong somewhere, say, in the back seat of a Chevrolet in high school. Rather, sin names the discovery, when confronted by the gospel, that my life has not been lived as a gift from God.

So when I discover that I am a creature in a story of God's good creation, I cannot help at the same time discovering that I am a sinner. So in an odd way I can only know I'm a sinner because I have been graced by God. I am able to confess my sin only because I know first I have been forgiven. This is but a reminder that forgiveness and repentance are not matters of priority but rather moments in a single practice made possible by Christ.

Learning to speak as a Christian is to acquire habits that will put me at odds with the world. Indeed, the very linguistic habit of describing the world as "world" is a practice. When Christians say "world" (Greek: *cosmos*) we are saying more than "universe" or "society" or "culture." We are saying something more like "Pentagon," that place where the principalities and powers are organized against God for the most noble of reasons.

Alasdair MacIntyre defines practice as:

> Any coherent and complex form of socially established cooperative human activity through which goods internal to that form of activity are realized in the course of trying to achieve those standards of excellence which are appropriate to, and partially definitive of, that form of activity, with the results that human powers to achieve excellence, and human conceptions of the ends and goods involved, are systematically extended.[6]

Our church leaders and educators need more skill in initiating people into theology as practice. At sixteen, Will's daughter enters a high school classroom. Odd, there are nozzles sticking up out of the desks. Someone plays with the nozzle while the teacher calls the roll. The teacher shouts, "Don't touch that! You want to blow us all up?"

Harriet had never heard of a classroom where one could be hurt.

Then the teacher begins to teach "Safety Rules." All week is spent on safety rules. You thought you knew how to pour liquid from one beaker to the next? No. There's a way we do it; the right way.

During the first week, someone behind Harriet asks the teacher, "What is that chart up on the wall? What do those strange numbers and words mean?"

"You're not ready for that," says the teacher. "Those are the sacred signs and symbols of our faith. You must wait for that."

At the end of the week there is an exam on the Safety Rules. If passed, each student receives a white robe, the liturgical garment of the faith, and goggles. "Now," says the teacher with a sense of expectancy, "now you are ready to enter the world of chemistry."

There is that day, later in the semester, when the teacher points to the chart and says, "Now you are at last ready to learn the secrets. I am going to teach you how to do things with these symbols that you have never done before. I am going to take you places you would never have gone, had you not had the good sense to take chemistry."

And the chemistry textbook. It's not just full of facts, figures, and formulae, but it also has pictures of heroes with short biographies, lives of folk who braved ignorance and injustice and taught us how to pasteurize milk. Saints!

Around the first of December, Harriet came in with a bag of groceries. Will watched as she reached in the bag and retrieved a package. "Heat activated deodorant," he heard Harriet read aloud.

She instinctively flipped the box over, saying to herself, "I wonder what this has in it. Something that reacts at about 98 degrees, I guess." And she read the list of chemicals in the deodorant.

As someone who is supposed to be in the conversion business, through inculcating the practices of an alien faith, Will stood in awe of that moment. Here was a miraculous transformation in the life of his daughter that had been worked in less than four months. That chemistry teacher did not just want to teach those students *about* chemistry; she wanted their souls. She did not just want to teach the students a few new words of chemical vocabulary, though that was part of the requisite patterns to be acquired; she wanted to inculcate a set of practices. Now, when Harriet looks out the window in the morning, she no longer sees the same world she saw four months ago. She is a chemist.

Acquiring practices is another way to say *conversion.* Something is gained; something is lost as well. Rarely are practices acquired without some cost, without detoxification, without letting go of the practices of one form of existence in order to embrace another. One of the reasons why we acquire habits and practices commensurate with being church is to be able to discern better the world in which we live. That is, to be able to discern that the world is at once God's but also still enemy territory. So we need to know how to describe the world appropriately. In other words, we need discriminating judgments about the actual world we confront. Like those Marine recruits at Parris Island, the inculcation of a set of truthful practices naturally makes one uneasy with one's former world.

The discriminating judgment we make about the world we confront is that it is one based on liberal political practices. The project of modernity has been to create a people who believe that they should have no story, except the story that they choose, as if they

had no story before they chose. Ironically, the notion
that it is possible to live by no story, other than the one
we have personally chosen, is also a story, which we did
not think up ourselves.

Late one night, on the fall Religious Life Retreat for
new students at the university, after a long discussion
of the differences between various religions, one student said in exasperation, "The thing that I hate about
you Christians is that you are always trying to convert
people."

[Widespread agreement in the group.]

"I think that you ought to leave people alone. After
all, religion is a very private matter between you and
God, and it's nobody else's business what you believe."

[Continued agreement in the group.]

But where did that student get the story that "religion is a very private matter between you and God"? She
did not come out of her mother's womb saying, "Religion is a very private matter between me and God."

Somebody had to tell her that story, *convert* her into
that rather silly idea. Knowing does not come naturally,
innately. Christians are not weird in that we try to
convert people. *Everyone* is, in some way or another, a
subject of conversion. All knowing, including the notion that "religion is a very private matter between me
and God," is externally, socially derived. Yet the amazing thing is that she cannot remember where it was that
she first heard, and was converted into, the idea that
"religion is a private matter between me and God."

There is some knowledge, there are some practices,
that are so thoroughly sanctioned by this culture, so
necessary to this economy, that they cease appearing

like acquired practices. They just seem normal, natural facts of life.

Where did we Americans get the story that our lives are our possessions, to make up whatever story we like and then to live that? We didn't think it up ourselves. No, it came to us through our society, our environment. We cannot free ourselves from such social determinism. The issue is not, "Will I live by an externally derived account of the world or not?" The question is, "Will the externally derived account of the world, which I live and die by, be true or false?"

The modern story of the self-fabricated individual is what most of us mean when we use the word *world*. Recalling this story's power over us reminds us that the division between church and world is not a division between a pure church and a pure world. The division between church and world runs through the soul of each of us, runs right down the aisle of every Christian congregation. That is why we need to be part of a church that makes us vulnerable to one another's stories. In listening to the stories of others, particularly to the stories of those who have not been the beneficiaries of the present economic and political order, we discover how strongly the world is part of us.

Christian education is not what happens in Sunday school. Rather, what is crucial for Christian formation is to have people engaged in activities through which they learn habits that shape them before they can name what the shaping is about. That is why Stanley thinks that nothing is better for helping Christians learn what it means to be Christian than teaching them how to play baseball. By throwing the ball, time and time again, one learns how to catch a ball. Catching a ball relates to the purposes of throwing people out at first base, and the practice of throwing people out at first base works within the whole pattern and purpose of playing baseball. All this is similar to the way that one becomes formed to be a Christian.

Therefore, when we say to people, "Do not lie," it is because they have already discovered that they are part of a community of truth that has learned how not to lie. Truth telling is not some heroic individual achievement; it is a gift of a truthful community that has initiated us into that family whereby liars like us are enabled to tell the truth.

Living the Truth

Consider George Bush's nomination of Clarence Thomas for the Supreme Court. George Bush told a terrific public lie when he said that Clarence Thomas was the best available person he could find for nomination to the Supreme Court. Of course, we all knew that was a lie, but few named it for what it was.

What George Bush should have said was that America is still a society that suffers from slavery and the development of racism as part of our slave experience. Accordingly it is important to appoint African Americans to positions of power where they can protect other African Americans from the racism that is still endemic to our society. The problem is that George Bush did not tell us that, not because he is venial, though he may be, but because the American people do not want to know the truth. We elect our leaders on the basis of whatever fantasies we happen to have at the moment, and they promise to confirm us in our fantasies.

Yet we as Christians are people who believe we want our leaders to tell us the truth, because without such a habit, no authority is possible. Without that truth, Christian community dies. That was the point we were trying to make in our reference to the story of Ananias and Sapphira in chapter 6 of *Resident Aliens*. There, we tried to say that our great desire for community must be prefaced by a desire for the truth because, without the truth, our communities become dangerous enclaves of deceit, another of our many defenses against having to look at ourselves honestly.

For example, a few years ago Stanley was asked to give a lecture at a university that was supported by the Southern Baptist's and that also had a business school. Since they were Southern Baptists, they wanted their business school to be "ethical." They had endowed an annual lectureship in business ethics, and Stanley was to give one of the initial lectures. He entitled his lecture, "Why Business Ethics is a Bad Idea." In the lecture he suggested that most business ethics courses are only forms of quandary ethics that focus on situations and as a result miss the real moral challenges before us.

Before the lecture there was a very pleasant obligatory dinner for faculty, the supporters of the lecture, and Stanley. During dinner the Associate Dean of the Business School had told Stanley that she was a member of a church in the city that had a membership between six and seven thousand and usually took in a hundred to two hundred new members each Sunday. After the lecture, she observed that she found the lecture pessimistic if not cynical. She suggested that surely there was something they could do to make their

business school more ethical. Stanley observed that he
certainly felt that there was, but they would have to
begin a good deal earlier than the business school. He
suggested before they let anyone join her church, they
ought to have the prospective member turn to the
congregation and publicly declare his or her income. "I
make $35,000 a year, and I want to be a member of this
church." "I make $185,000 a year, and I want to be a
member of this church." "I make $65,000 a year, and I
want to be a member of this church." She observed that
they could not do that. He asked, "Why?" And she said,
"Well, that's private." All Stanley could think of was:
Where are the fundamentalists when we need them?

The early church seems to have known nothing,
given what happened to Ananias and Sapphira, of the
distinction between the public and the private. The
early church was quite clear that if you have money,
your salvation is in trouble. Yet because we refuse as
Christians to tell one another what we make, we become condemned to live out that loneliness that is so
intrinsic to the capitalist society. The truth of the matter
is that as Christians today, we would rather tell one
another, if it was absolutely necessary, what we do in
our bedrooms before we'd have to tell one another
what we make a year.

That is, of course, the reason why the practice of
Christian marriage has become so difficult in the world
we inhabit. Even in marriage between Christians we
meet as strangers unable to tell one another the truth.
Yet Christians believe that nothing is more important
in marriage than truthfulness.

Yet people often lie most readily in marriage exactly
because they fear losing the intimacy they have

achieved to that point. They know that nothing can kill the fires of passion quicker than truth. That is why we Christians assert that marriages must be sustained by more fundamental practices than simply how they enrich the interpersonal relationship between two people. Marriage is subservient to discipleship. Our marriages are ultimately significant only as a means of supporting each of us in our ministry, including the ministries of childrearing, conversion of the young, protection of the old. We think marriage is a place where Christians are able to be truthful with one another because marriage is more determinative than their immediate feelings.

Whether Christians in their marriages can be truthful depends on marriage not being isolated from the community. Christians are asked to have their marriages witnessed before the whole community where that community can then hold them to promises they made when they didn't know what they were doing. How could you ever know what you were doing when you promised another to be faithful for a lifetime? But exactly because we promise to be faithful for a lifetime we know we can risk telling one another the truth, since the bond of marriage is more determinative than our personal satisfaction at any one time. That allows Christians to be married with joy.

There is an intimate relationship between truth and nonviolence. Christian truth telling is nonviolent exactly because it refuses to let the lies rest. Here we see again how the church we want cannot be sectarian exactly because it must be about the evangelical exposure of the lies that underwrite the violence of the surrounding society.

One of the examples Stanley uses to illustrate this is to ask whether we ought to keep a gun in church. That we do not keep a gun in church is an interesting habit, yet we have failed to notice its significance. We have theology students who serve in western North Carolina in small rural churches. In some of these mountain valleys, you never know when a motorcycle gang might drive through and rush into the church, screaming, "We're going to rape and kill all of you!"

Wouldn't it be prudent to keep an AK-47 in a gun rack, readily available underneath the cross? The minister could grab it and blow the marauders away, thereby demonstrating that ministers really are macho and that the church is always ready to defend itself.

But people feel squeamish about keeping a gun under the cross. Why?

Is it not because we believe that the church has more powerful weapons than a gun to confront the world's violence? We have such powerful weapons because we have practices of truthfulness within the church that come from the language that we have learned to speak—such as confession of sin—that helps us maintain peaceable habits that confront the world's violence.

An Interview with Stanley Hauerwas

ALEXANDER: You observe that the church in North America exists in a consumer-driven market environment. You say that this is a problem because "the called church has become the voluntary church, whose primary characteristic is that the congregation is friendly." Isn't it important for congregations to be perceived as inviting and willing to accept and care for people—warts and all?

HAUERWAS: No! No! I don't want God to accept me the way I am. I want God to transform me, to make me perfect. Of course, the church rightly says to people, "We want you to know the joy of the life of what it means to worship God." But you're going to need a lot of transformation to be part of this kind of community because your life cannot remain the same when you become a member of the church of Jesus Christ. All your desires and loyalties must be directed to the worship of God, and that means, for example, you're not going to be a good American anymore. You're not going to believe that church and flag go easily together. And it may well change your friendships. You may not be able to be friends with some because their way of life is corrupting.

I don't believe in the "you are accepted" ideology. It is a way of our escaping the necessity of judgment on ourselves and a way to ensure we will have shallow souls. I'm not for accepting people the way they are. As Mark Twain observed, "About the worst advice you can give anyone is to be themselves."

ALEXANDER: Have you seen congregations at work that embody what you mean? What goes on in the life of such congregations?

HAUERWAS: I think such churches are led by a pastor who preaches and serves the sacraments in a way that presumes that without God none of this makes any sense. The problem with so much of the church growth literature is that many of the strategies offered are based upon atheism. These are techniques which work irrespective of whether people are deeply formed in faith in God's work through the resurrection of Jesus of Nazareth.

What could be more important than helping churches rediscover the fact that there's nothing more critical for the world than for a body of people to set aside time in their lives to do nothing but worship God? . . . An example is a young pastor I met who told me, "They are putting terrible pressure on me to place yellow ribbons on my church and what should I do?" I suggested we seek the counsel of a more experienced pastor, who said, "The problem with the yellow ribbon is that it's too ambiguous as a Christian symbol for what we care about. Why don't we put up crosses?"

I think the church, for all its accommodated status, still creates spaces that make that kind of witness possible. Where people worship God, God uses us in extraordinary ways. My hope is not finally in an accommodated church, but in God who uses even the accommodated church for possibilities of witness that we haven't even imagined. God finds ways to force us to be faithful.

ALEXANDER: You write that "we live in societies . . . formed by the assumption that there is literally nothing for which it is worth dying." Are you calling Christians to engage in battle? If so, to what end?

HAUERWAS: I am calling Christians to battle—against war, against practices based on atheism, against all that invites us to be indifferent—we just cannot kill in that battle as that would belie the reason we fight. We fight so that God will be glorified. In the process, we hope that other people will be attracted to the wonder of what it means to worship a God that gives our lives a sense of participation in the adventure we call Kingdom. One of the most important things Will Willimon and I said in *Resident Aliens* was that nothing is more indicative of liberalism's corruption of Christians than the assumption that we can have children who will not have to suffer for our convictions. That obviously produces a view that there is nothing worth living and/or dying for.

ALEXANDER: There has been much talk lately about family values and the importance of the family. You wrote in *Community of Character* about the family as the primary focus for Christian witness. Yet you gave a sermon entitled "Hating Mothers as the Way to Peace." Are these claims contradictory?

HAUERWAS: I don't believe that the family is the primary locus of Christian witness. The church is the primary locus of Christian witness. And the first enemy of the family is the church. The church reminds people that their destiny is not carried through familial continuity but by a body of people who are dedicated to the worship of God in a world that knows not God.

You can be sure that Christians no longer believe that our witness to God is truthful, just to the extent that they make the family a fetish. I am, therefore, not "pro family." But I do think that the most determinative moral experience that people have in modernity is the recognition that they need to be responsible for their children. Parents don't choose their children. Children are a gift, and parents are called to live a way of life that makes them better than they otherwise would be.[7]

Christians are embedded in a whole set of revolutionary, subversive practices, while failing to notice their significance. Simply to say that Christians are those who always go to church on Sundays may be a more significant practice than we know. Are there things that Christians should not do on Sunday? That question has been lost, but we think it needs to be found again. In a world where work is integral to worth, where the majority of our neighbors see Sunday morning as a time to go to the lake or to mow their grass, just getting up, getting dressed, and going to church becomes a sort of nonviolent protest, a way of saying, "We want a different world than the one you serve." Just teaching our children that we go to church, without being able to explain the "deeper significance," might have immense political significance.

"Dr. Willimon, could you recommend a book that explains what Presbyterians believe?" he asked.

"Why would I have such a book?" Will asked. "That's the trouble with you Presbyterians, you're always reading some book. You ought to be like us Methodists and feel a warm tingle down your back."

"Well, back in Grand Rapids, everybody we knew went to church. It's what we always did on Sunday mornings. So when I came here to the university, I did what I always did out of habit. On Sunday, I got up, I got dressed, I went to church. But I noticed that I was the only person leaving my dorm. And then there were these questions."

"Questions?"

"Yea, questions, good natured at first. But lately, this guy in my fraternity jumped on me yesterday saying, 'What makes you think that you're so special, just because you go to church? I saw you at the house party last weekend. You're no better than the rest of us. Why do you go to church?'

"So I need a book to explain who I am and what I'm doing. Nobody ever asked me to explain being a Presbyterian before," he said.

Will said, "Wonderful! Duke University has succeeded in making even Presbyterians interesting!"

Little, habitual, seemingly insignificant practices like going to church, not having sex with people to whom we are not married, not telling a racist joke, and telling the truth take on new significance in the present struggle.

Or again, consider the practice of the church year and why it is that Christians ought not to celebrate Thanksgiving and Mother's Day in the church. We cannot because Thanksgiving for us is known only eucharistically and therefore ought not to be co-opted as a national holiday. Even now we hear of a United Methodist pastor who may have to leave his church after refusing to allow Santa Claus to visit his church on the Sunday before Christmas. It seemed a ridiculous response, on the part of his congregation, to make such a fuss over their pastor's hatred of Santa Claus. Yet, as the pastor told us, "Looking back upon the argument, I think they had the good sense to see that I was (even unknown to me) attacking everything they believed in. They would not have been so angry with me if it had been a matter of no consequence."

We need pastors with the skills to analyze our present practices, to ask which social order these practices serve, and to lead us to distinctively Christian habits.

CHAPTER FIVE

Disciplines of Discipleship

Joyful Aliens

Some are offended that we use the term *resident aliens*, fearing that we are in some way beating up on Hispanic immigrants. These observers are people whose chief aim is to help immigrants to feel like good Americans.

We have no problem with immigrants feeling like immigrants. Indeed, we heard a Mexican American woman being interviewed on public radio the day before Thanksgiving. She told about her fears upon arriving in the United States. The place was so strange. She feared for her children. One day in November, her husband brought home a turkey, a huge turkey given to him by his boss as a Thanksgiving present.

"It looked so ugly and white," said the woman. "I refused to cook it."

"But it's American!" said the husband. "Everyone in America eats like this. This is what they call 'Thanksgiving.'"

"But I don't know if we want to be Americans," she said. "I think we need to be careful. We need to wait and find out what all this means."

"It's just a turkey," said the husband. "What harm can eating a turkey do to us?"

"I cooked the turkey," she said. "The next day, like good Americans, we all sat around the table with that huge bird. My husband ate some, the children nibbled a bit at it, but I refused to eat a bite."

This woman knows in her heart of hearts that something large is at stake in the way we eat. She knows enough to be wary of this new culture. First it's a nibble of turkey here, and a nibble there, and the next thing you know your son is in banking.

Aliens (Greek: *paroikos* and *parpidamos*) is the chief metaphor employed by 1 Peter to describe a Christian's relationship to the surrounding social order. (We are indebted here to Miroslav Volf, Fuller Theological Seminary, for this insight.) *Alien* is a central self-understanding of Christians from the second century onward. It was employed by the Anabaptists, Augustine, Zinzendorf and, more recently, by Dietrich Bonhoeffer, *The Cost of Discipleship;, Jim Wallis, Sojourners*, and eloquently by William Stringfellow in his *An Ethic for Christians and Other Aliens in a Strange Land* (1973). We were surprised, after *Resident Aliens* was published that we did not recall Stringfellow's book. Upon reading that book again, it is humbling to see how he dealt with these themes twenty years before us.

Abraham left his country and kindred (Genesis 12:1). His heirs became "aliens in the land of Egypt" (Leviticus 19:34). The Fourth Gospel says that Jesus "came to what was his own, and his own people did not accept him" (John 1:11).

Homelessness has become a central metaphor for our age. Do we focus on the plight of the homeless, not only because homeless people living on the streets are a sign of the terrible failure of this society, but also because, in the homeless, each of us sees an image of self?

Catholic novelist Walker Percy explores this free-floating, sometimes desperate, usually ill-defined sense of homelessness in his novels. In a famous essay he asks:

> Why is a man apt to feel bad in a good environment, say suburban Short Hills, New Jersey, on an ordinary Wednesday afternoon? Why is the same man apt to feel good in a very bad environment, say an old hotel on Key Largo during a hurricane?
>
> Why is it that a man riding a good commuter train from Larchmont to New York, whose needs and drives are satisfied, who has a good home, loving wife and family, good job, often feels bad without knowing why?
>
> Why is the good life which men have achieved in the twentieth century so bad that only news of world catastrophes, assassinations, plane crashes, mass murders, can divert one from the sadness of ordinary mornings?
>
> What does a man do when he finds himself living after an age has ended and he can no longer understand himself because the theories of the new age are not yet known, and so everything is upside down, people feeling bad when they should feel good, good when they should feel bad?[1]

More recently, "Generation X" novelist Douglas Coupland questions if this generation is so far away from ever having had a home that it cannot even be said to be "lost." One of his characters in *Life After God*, speaking with some of his young adult friends, says:

"I know you guys think my life is some big joke—that it's going nowhere. But I'm happy. And its not like I'm lost or anything. We're all too f . . . . . g middle class to ever be lost. Lost means you had faith or something to begin with and the middle class never really had any of that. So we can never be lost. And you tell *me*, Scout— what is it we end up being, then—what exactly *is* it we end up being then—instead of being lost?"[2]

Accuse us of providing theological justification to sociological realities if you will, but we consider it a happy gift of God that here, at the end of a millennium, increasing numbers of Christians in North America sense that something is wrong; they feel lost, cast adrift, afloat on a sea of uncertainty, homeless. Undoubtedly, the Petrine designation of early Christians as aliens and sojourners arose in a situation in which baptism pushed one to the periphery of the dominant order, not so much on the basis of baptism's demands, but rather because the dominant order is intolerant. It is unaccepting of anyone who fails to bow before the altar inscribed with the claim that all intolerance must be rejected except for the intolerance that says we must be equally tolerant of all claims.

Celsus was among the first of these critics of whom we have record. In the second century, Celsus accused Christians of glorifying their differences from the dominant Greco-Roman culture out of a hate for classical philosophy and art. Christians, according to this first of the cultured disposers and despisers of Christianity, were weird simply because they loved to be weird. Our rebuttal to Celsus is that a Christian's distance from society depends, in great part, upon the society. How open is that particular society to those who worship the true and living God of Israel and the church? Any distance between Christians and the surrounding world is not due to our hate of the world. We have, after all, been taught as Christians that this world is God's creation and possession. The world we reject is *our* world, the world we loved and its gods to whom we bowed. Our distance as Christians is not so much distance from our sinful neighbors in the world but rather from the world in us. Any distance is due, not to our hate of the world, but to our love of God.

After condemning resident aliens of sectarian revisionism, John S. McClure warns preachers that following other resident aliens would lead to preaching that is narrow and exclusive, preaching that,

> invites people to live in suspicion of the world around them and to adopt a very narrow and particular definition of what is culturally consummate with the gospel message. . . . This tendency can lead to an attitude of fear, superiority, prejudice, or even hatred of the world.[3]

Ardent cultural accommodationists always regard the church as "narrow" and the world as "wide."

When Will was in Australia, where somewhere less than 20 percent of the population is identified as Christian, there was a news story about a pentecostal church in Sydney that had been vandalized for the second time in a month. Earlier, someone had started a fire at the church. Now someone had shoved a fire hose in the window of the church, ruining the contents of the building. The church was located in a small business

The authors of Resident Aliens *do not call on the church to become an exclusive sect which gathers in self-righteous judgment on the world. Rather they call on the church to become what it was originally—a "colony of heaven," a colony that challenges a world it loves and is willing to die for but not conform to.*

Is it realistic to hope that such a church could emerge out of the present one? Recently a Toronto church was looking for a new minister. But first it worked on a mission statement—a manifesto—a purpose. Among other things it said: "We want a leader who will dare us to take the risks of the gospel seriously."

That kind of church may indeed be crucified. But it will never be boring.[4]

—The Toronto Star, June 22, 1991

center, so when the vandals flooded the church, they also flooded the surrounding businesses.

The owner of a florist shop next door to the church complained, "No one told me, when I rented this shop, that I would be next door to a church. I'm really quite upset with having to have a business next to a church. First the fire; now this. It's no place for a respectable business like mine. All of my stock has been ruined."

The reporter asked a police spokesperson, "Do you think this is anti-religious violence here?"

"Anti-religious? No. This was a church," said the policeman.

"But two incidents in one month. Doesn't that seem like something is happening here, like someone is trying to say something to this church?"

"No. It's just two random acts of vandalism," said the policeman.

What impresses us is that, if these acts had been perpetrated against a mosque, a synagogue, or an Afri-

can American church, *everyone* would have called it
racist, or anti-religious, for these groups are clearly at
odds with the dominant order and are periodically
attacked for that reason. There is as yet a failure to
recognize that churches are increasingly finding themselves in exactly the same situation as our neighborhood mosque.

Also interesting is the refusal of the Sydney police
to admit that this was indeed anti-Christian violence.
To be fair, perhaps the police are unaccustomed to a
church that is so interesting, so clear in its life and
message that the surrounding culture clearly knows
that it is a threat! A church, in Sydney or elsewhere, is
torched or flooded ought to see this act as the world's
validation of its ministry!

We live in wonderful times. The Christian faith has
always done quite well during times of cultural chaos
and the complete disintegration of society (otherwise
known, for example, as downtown LA). Baptism both
names our estrangement as alienation from God and
encourages us to embrace a new culture and community (church) that gives us something worth being
estranged for and helps us to enjoy being weird.

As aliens we are not trying to make the world worse
than it is for the church to recover its integrity. The
world is quite bad enough as it is without our encour-
agement to be worse. Indeed, we recognize that much
good from the world can come to the church if the
church is appropriately alien. The God we worship as
Christians is in the world, and we should not be surprised that we often discover there people and practices more faithful than we are in the church.

Christians do not need to make the world worse than it is for us to regain our integrity. Rather, all we have to do is to be what God has made us, for as Christians we've been made part of a story that the world cannot know unless we are embodied in that story. The world cannot know that God has chosen to redeem the world through the Jews unless we Christians witness to that.

Christians are not first called to be aliens. Jesus calls us to be *witnesses* "in Jerusalem, in all Judea and Samaria, and to the ends of the earth" (Luke 1:8). It is interesting and sobering that the Greek word for "witness" is the same root as our word *martyr*. Jesus has not called us to hunker down behind the barricades but rather to "Go . . . and make disciples of all nations, baptizing them . . . teaching them" (Matthew 28:19).

Yet it is important for the church as witness to have something to say that is more interesting than what the world says. We gave the world credit, because in part the world mostly ignores us for having so little to say that the world cannot hear as well elsewhere. When church becomes Rotary, church will lose because Rotary serves lunch and meets at a convenient hour of the week!

We are called, even in one of the most exclusionary books of the New Testament, to live "honorably among the Gentiles . . . so that they may see your honorable deeds and glorify God when he comes to judge" (1 Peter 2:12). Our worry about the condition of the church is more than concern for internal health. Our concern arises out of our commitment to be witnesses. The church exists, not for itself but to save the world, to "proclaim the mighty acts of him who called you out of darkness into his marvelous light" (1 Peter 2:9). So the question is not *whether* we shall live as Christians in this world, for that is no option for us. Rather, the question is, Now that God has entered this world as Jesus the Christ, *how* then shall we live? It is a question not only of ecclesial survival but also of missional, evangelistic significance.

One of our students came under the influence of a sect that was rumored to be working on campus. His parents called Will, frantic to rescue their son from the dominance of this demanding separatist group. The group was completely monopolizing the young man's life.

When Will finally met with him, they talked about his experience with the group. When Will asked, he told him that he had grown up in a Lutheran church in the Midwest, that his parents had been active in the church all their lives.

"Then how on earth, I must ask, could you become involved in this strange fringe group?" Will asked.

"Well, it all started on the first Sunday I visited them. When I walked into their church, I saw black people, white people, people of every shade of the rainbow. You could feel the love. Our church had always *preached* this sort of loving fellowship to me. But I had never seen it until I walked into that group. I said to myself, 'This is the church I've always heard about but have never seen until now.' "

Will waited some time before he asked him other questions.

And thus we come to the question of discipline.

Growing the Church, the Old-Fashioned Way

What would it mean for our church to be a disciplined community? Here we want to juxtapose our account of the church with that offered in most of the church-growth movement. There's a wonderful story about Clarence Jordan, who visited an integrated church in the Deep South. Jordan was surprised to find a relatively large church so thoroughly integrated, not only black and white but also rich and poor. Jordan asked the old hillbilly preacher, "How did you get the church this way?"

"What way?" the preacher asked. Jordan went on to explain his surprise at finding a church so integrated, and in the South, too. The preacher said, "Well, when our preacher left our small church, I went to the Deacons and said, 'I'll be the preacher.' The first Sunday as preacher, I opened the book and read, 'As many of you as has been baptized into Jesus has put on Jesus and there is no longer any Jews or Greeks, slaves or free, males or females, because you is all one in Jesus.'

"Then I closed the book and said, 'If you one with Jesus, you one with all kind of folks. And if you ain't, you ain't.' " Jordan asked what happened after that.

"Well," the preacher said, "the Deacons took me into the back room and told me they didn't want to hear that kind of preaching no more." Jordan asked what he did. "I fired them Deacons," the preacher roared.

"Then what happened?" asked Jordan.

"Well," said the old hillbilly preacher, "I preached that church down to four. Not long after that, it grew and grew and grew. And I found out that revival sometimes don't mean bringin' people in but gettin' people out that don't love Jesus."

We admit it; we're both Methodists. Methodism is historically big on evangelism, not as a program for church growth but as a way to have a disciplined community.

Methodism after all is a movement that by accident became a church. Wesley never sought to set up a separate denomination from the Church of England, but rather to lead a movement of disciplined reforms within the Church of England. That is why Methodism is never at home ecclesially. We're not particularly Protestant, nor are we particularly Catholic. Accordingly, Methodism only makes sense as a people longing for unity through the discovery of meeting one another as people disciplined by Christ.

Our colleague Richard Heitzenrater makes this wonderfully clear in his *Wesley and the People Called Methodists*. Methodism was an extraordinary combination of the willingness to preach to the "underclasses" of England in the eighteenth century. And just as important was the formation of those people into "Classes." Those Classes arose from the need of the Methodists to collect money for the paying of the debt for building houses where Methodists could gather. It was suggested that everyone in the Society called Methodist contribute a penny a week, which had already been done at the Foundry Society, in order to assist the poor. But someone protested that not everyone in the Society could afford that much. Accordingly, Captain Foy suggested that the Methodist Society be divided into groups of twelve, each with a leader who would be responsible for turning in twelve pence a week, making up themselves whatever they could not collect. He volunteered to take as his group the eleven poorest.[5]

Accordingly, Methodism began as a disciplined body of people to aid one another and the poor. Its theology of sanctification and perfection found its soteriology in these Classes, through which Methodists made their lives vulnerable to one another so that they might move on to perfection. That is why Methodists, and in particular Wesley, always maintained that they were not saying anything different from that for which classical Christianity had always stood. Rather, what they sought was the discovery of practices that they could hold in common, what made them Christians. In effect, the Methodists of the eighteenth century were the Black Muslims of their day. They covenanted to be disciplined in terms of both their theological language and the practices commensurate with that language to be a people who would not be forced into lives of degradation simply because they were poor.

In his codification of the examination process in order to be a member of the Methodist Society, Wesley spelled out the rules for membership: "In order to join a Society, persons were required to demonstrate only one condition: 'a desire to flee from the wrath to come, to be saved from their sins.' Those who desired to continue in the Society, however, were expected 'to evidence their desire of salvation. First by doing no harm. . . . Secondly, by doing good. . . . Thirdly, by depending upon all the ordinances of God.'"[6] These rules were fleshed out with specific examples. These examples drew on Wesley's experience of actually having to exclude people from the Societies. Thus, for example, two had been excluded for cursing and swearing, two for habitual sabbath breaking, seventeen for drunkenness, two for retailing liquor, three for quarrelling and brawling, one for beating his wife, three for habitual, willful lying and railing and evil speaking, one for idleness and laziness, and twenty-nine for lightness and carelessness.

Methodism grew. It grew because it offered salvation by saving people from the degradation of the general habits of eighteenth-century English society. Of course, the Methodists reflected as much as reacted against the society in which they found themselves. But our point is that here people were embedded into God's salvation because they were given a new way of life that saved them from the expectations of their social order.

As Heitzenrater points out, the irony of Wesley's attempt to reform the church by spreading scriptural holiness is that it resulted in increasing self-conscious identity among Methodists, which also intensified pressures for separation from the Church of England.[7] This separation became peculiarly powerful in the American context, as Methodism became an end in itself. As a result, Methodism became part of the Protestant schism, showing its unfaithfulness by being an end in itself rather than the disciplined attempt to establish a people of holiness who long for union with one another.

Methodists and other forms of alien life have resources in their tradition that can call us back to faithfulness by offering us skills of resistance against the powers of our day. Such resources are simple matters, such as learning again how to confess our sins by naming them. This comes through simple acts of learning to stand together and confess our faith as people

who realize that we have been made what we are by
the faithfulness of the past.

> I believe in God, the Father Almighty,
>   creator of heaven and earth.

> I believe in Jesus Christ, his only Son, our Lord,
>   who was conceived by the Holy Spirit,
>   born of the Virgin Mary,
>   suffered under Pontius Pilate,
>   was crucified, died, and was buried;
>   he descended to the dead.
>   On the third day he rose again;
>   he ascended into heaven,
>   is seated at the right hand of the Father,
>   and will come again to judge the living and the dead.

> I believe in the Holy Spirit,
>   the holy catholic church,
>   the communion of saints,
>   the forgiveness of sins,
>   the resurrection of the body
>   and the life everlasting. Amen.

When we confess such creeds we become part of the
practices of the church across the centuries and are
unified with the saints who have gone before and the
saints among us so that we can stand against the forces
of this world. The creeds are not simply "statements of
belief." Rather, through learning to speak this language
we find we have the resources to resist the world. That
is the reason why resident aliens refuse to separate
doctrine from life, but believe indeed that a people who
rightly know how to confess that Jesus Christ is our

Lord is also a people who worry about what it would mean to tell the truth, not only to one another but also to the world. Such a people, of course, must be possessed by the virtues of humility and hope, because we realize that the truth is not ours. Humility is not false modesty but rather the confidence that comes from knowing that we have been made more than we could be through the care provided by our brothers and sisters in Christ.

Despite its accommodated nature, we still find great power in our church. For example, Stanley remembers graphically a wonderful Sunday in his church. It was Lay Sunday. Stanley despises Lay Sunday because it is so clerical and condescending. But that Sunday three of our laity testified as part of our worship. The first was a young mother, wife of an intern, who had three children. She had been raised Roman Catholic, in Alabama. Now a Methodist, she told us that her life mainly involved bringing up their children as part of the church by teaching them the stories of the Bible, by bringing them to church to be reminded of their baptism, and helping them learn what it means to be a member of the Body of Christ. She said, "I know that is not much, but right now I think that's what God wants me to do.

Next was a young man, not a particularly remarkable person. He had a job in a state agency—a bureaucrat. He said that he has to come to church because he has to be reminded that Christians do not lie. He has to be reminded of that because he said every day at his job he is surrounded with lies, and it's so hard to resist not becoming part of the system of lies. So he comes each Sunday in hopes of renewing his speech so he will not lie on the job. This may not contribute to his advancement, but he would rather be a Christian.

Finally, an elderly widow in the congregation testified that for her Christianity and quilting were closely connected. She told how during World War II she had served in the Navy as a cryptographer to break down the codes of the Japanese navy. She said she'd really never thought during that time about the people they were fighting. However, now she ran an international quilting bee that attracted many graduate student spouses from the nearby university. In the process, she had met several young Japanese women who were anxious to learn the art of quilting, and through them she had discovered Japanese Christianity. In the process she had gained a sense of the horror of what it meant for us to drop the atomic bomb on Japan.

She continued that even though it may not seem like much, she found her quilting a way to be tied to Christians around the world. She noted that, though it might be silly, the quilters thought they ought to do something to suggest that commitment. So a number of the quilting societies encouraged their members to do 3′ × 5′ quilts and come to Washington and surround the Pentagon with their quilts. That was the way she made a contribution to the world as a Christian. All Stanley could think was, "Thank you Jesus," for reminding us that close to death though we may be, you raise up life among us.

What we require today is a way to make lives like these the center of our Classes—that we will be a disciplined people capable of holding one another to account so that we give to the world the honesty and humility of the gospel. There is a connection between being a sober and disciplined people and one capable of confessing, "I believe in God, the Father Almighty." Christian morality is not a morality separate from our practice of confession, since our lives are meant to be holy lives and capable of making such confessions.

We seek not to be many but to be true. If we are a truthful community, we believe we will attract many. But God does not need many for God's kingdom to be manifest—for finally it is not about us; it is about God. So, yes, we want to share the good news of what God has done for our salvation.

One may overlook Hauerwas' confusion of churchly support for political democracy with an unwitting distortion of kingdom-of-God credentials and ask whether theonomy then remains the only politically acceptable option for the Christian community. Most evangelical friends of democracy do not confuse democracy with the kingdom of God but welcome its limited role for government and its emphasis that the ground of religious freedom and of other human rights transcends national determination.

What one misses in Hauerwas is a clear indication of why Christians must live responsibly in two communities. He rejects social withdrawal from the public arena and argues for selective service with an emphasis on priorities. But what is to stimulate Christians governed by the sermon on the mount to move beyond interpersonal concerns to shared public concerns? And is not truth—universally valid truth—a concern as fundamental to the Church's public involvement as are forgiveness, hope, and peace? In any case the Church has a mandate for public evangelism. What in Hauerwas' view is her mandate for public involvement? If selective service is a matter of secular prudence screened through Christian values, what relation, if any, does public involvement hold to

> *the coming of God's kingdom¿ Is public involvement only*
> *optional¿ Or ought Christians to be involved to the limit of*
> *their ability and competence, and if so, why¿*
>
> *Precisely as the true Church the Christian community is to*
> *be reminded that she must not hide her light or withhold her*
> *salt from the world. She is to warn the world, as I see it, that*
> *law and justice have their ultimate ground and defining source*
> *in the transcendent will of the self-revealing God, to proclaim*
> *to the world the universal criteria by which Christ will judge*
> *men and nations at his return, is to encourage society to judge*
> *itself anticipatively by the divine commandments that*
> *threaten impenitent humanity, is to exemplify in her own*
> *ranks what faithful obedience to the Lord of the Church and*
> *of history implies, and is to exhibit to the world the blessings*
> *of serving the true and living God.*[8]
>
> —Carl F. Henry

For us, evangelism means bringing people into Christian disciplines to save them from the world. It doesn't mean calling them from service in the world, though it might mean that some of the services would get tough. Rather, it means that they will have the disciplines necessary to be in the world as Christians, which is our service to the world.

Consider the relationship between discipline and friendship. To be disciplined means to make our lives vulnerable to friends. That is, we need people who will tell us the truth about ourselves. Stanley tells people as often as he can that he is a pacifist because he is obviously a very violent person from Texas. By creating expectations in others, even though he often deeply dislikes what they think pacifism entails, their expectations will keep him faithful to what he knows is true. One way to become a pacifist is to go out and tell everyone that you are. Then, in the arguments and challenges that follow, you will end up becoming as you profess. You start to resemble your arguments.

In other words, the Christian life means, in baptism, to put oneself in the context of other lives that can make us more than we could ever be by ourselves. Discipline is just that kind of vulnerability. Discipline means having certain alternatives simply excluded from our lives, by being put in Christian habits that render the alternatives impractical. Therefore, Christians are not tempted to adultery or suicide because those are not alternatives for us. We use those words to mark off decisions that never happen in the church. Of course they happen, and that is the reason why we are happy to have ways of discriminatingly responding to those events.

Remember, we resident aliens are in a fight. If you're in a fight, you need to be part of a disciplined people who can sustain you in the fight. In other words, you need to have gone through boot camp, which has trained your attention by teaching you a new language, the way the Marines teach you a way to tell time. Thus you will have the means of helping the world know it is the world, because you do not tell time the way the world tells time.

Discipline isn't something like will power, to do things we do not want to do. Rather, discipline is the acquisition of habits through which we would not do anything other than what we are delightfully doing. Christian discipline gives us joy, because through discipline we acquire power that otherwise we would not have had.

THE DOOR

INTERVIEWS

William Willimon and Stanley Hauerwas

DOOR: What does it mean to be a "resident alien" in this culture?

WILLIMON: It means that the Gospel is weird and, if you believe the Gospel, then you will be weird. If you believe the Gospel, you feel yourself in collision with the most widely held and deeply affirmed values of this society. I remember a story Jim Wallis [editor of *Sojourners Magazine*] told about his childhood. His parents were Fundamentalists and did not want Jim to go to the movies. When he had been a teenager awhile, he searched the movie guide trying to find a suitable movie to break the ice. He invited a girl from his church youth group to go with him to see *The Sound of Music*. He announced this to his parents and they said nothing. He thought he was home free. As he was leaving for his date to see *The Sound of Music*, his father stood in the door and said, with tears streaming down his face, "Please don't do this to us. This is against everything we believe in." Jim Wallis went to the movie anyway. What stands out in his mind is how silly the whole movie business was, especially in view of what is going on today. He believes there really are things to stand in the door over. A "resident alien" is someone who stands in the door of culture. If we don't do that, then it's a little nibble here and a little nibble there, and one day you wake up and you are at the Republican National Convention. Stanley and I do believe in the peculiarity of the Gospel. Being on a university campus, I am continually amazed at how the simplest little everyday Christian stuff is considered radical and weird.

DOOR: From what you have just said and from reading your book, it sounds like you are saying that the Church should quit trying to influence society through the government.

WILLIMON: What we are saying is that when you work with the government, you should do it like porcupines make love . . . very carefully. . . .

DOOR: One of the criticisms of your book is that it is socially irresponsible to suggest that the Church quit trying to influence the government.

WILLIMON: Politicians love words like "responsibility." But once you accept something like the Gulf War in the name of political responsibility, then everything else goes down easy. We are the Church, and maybe the most "responsible" thing we could have done in the war with Iraq is to have said, "Here is a country ruled by a despot. We'd better make that a major area of evangelism this year, so we are going to send 1,000 missionaries to Iraq." That would have screwed up things beautifully. The government would have said, "How are we going to bomb Iraq with all those damn missionaries running loose?" And we would have said, "That's your problem. But if you hit one of our missionaries, there's going to be hell to pay." That is political responsibility from the viewpoint of the Church.

DOOR: The Church thumbs its nose at the government?

WILLIMON: The Church doesn't understand the government. President Clinton was approached by a black woman who said, "Please save black males for us." He said he would do what he could. Save black males? How is he going to do that? Does he have some kind of program for that? We don't understand this business of Caesar going down in the ghetto and saying, "It's OK, people, we've got you under control. I am going up to the White House in Washington and I'm going to work on some stuff for you." That is what we don't understand. That is what we don't want to have any part of.

DOOR: So you want Christians out of politics.

HAUERWAS: No problem with Christians being in politics, as long as they are there as Christians.

DOOR: Now you sound like Jerry Falwell.

HAUERWAS: I like a lot of what Jerry Falwell says. I do. He just happens to be an idolater when it comes to America. He's just screwed up about what a Christian politician is, but other than that he has some good stuff. . . . My feeling about Washington is like my feeling about the Vatican. Try to ignore it. Someday it will topple by its own weight.

DOOR: This is getting depressing.

HAUERWAS: You ought to be depressed.

HAUERWAS: I was speaking at a banquet in New York. Ed Koch was there, and I was seated next to the Episcopal bishop of New York. . . . The bishop told me that Ed Koch had called him to ask if each Episcopal church in the Manhattan area could take in seven homeless people every night. [The bishop] responded by saying, "I certainly will not do that for you, mayor. That is just trying to relieve your responsibility as the mayor to provide public housing for these people. We are certainly not going to take the monkey off your back." I told [the bishop] that he missed the voice of Jesus in Mayor Koch, that Christians have an obligation of hospitality, and Mayor Koch was just trying to remind [the bishop] of that. I told the bishop that the real reason he told the mayor "no" probably had more to do with the fact that most Anglican churches in Manhattan don't want to have homeless people with them at night.

DOOR: Why do we have the feeling you are not one of the bishop's favorite people?

HAUERWAS: He turned his back and wouldn't talk to me the rest of the evening.

DOOR: What about the Church and Jesus? We see a lot of churches taking responsibility for a number of social ills, but what about the churches' spiritual lives? What about their relationship with Jesus? We haven't heard either one of you address that issue.

WILLIMON: The question of Jesus has become an interesting question again. When you have ministers running around with briefcases and daytimers, the question of intimacy with Jesus is a very appropriate question. Countless laypeople have said to me, "We want a spiritual leader." I ask them what they mean by that, and they tell me very directly. They are tired of their minister talking only about the weather and sports. They are frustrated when the minister comes to visit you after you have been told you have cancer and spends 10 minutes talking about how you are doing and then leaves. People want a minister who talks about God—who loves to talk about God.

HAUERWAS: I was sick a couple of years ago, and a minister visited me and said very nicely, "How are we doing today?"

DOOR: Uh-oh.

HAUERWAS: I grabbed him and said, "I am hurting like hell, and if you don't pray for me right now, then get out of this damn room." I needed a person of power who was ready to claim the power of God for me. [If I'm in the hospital,] I don't need some kind of "tingling mass of availability" who hasn't the slightest idea why he is there. The reason there is so much adultery amongst ministers today is that they are so lonely. They need to feel some power. Adultery is a form of power. This epidemic of adultery is going to continue as long as ministers don't trust God. God transforms people's lives. The Eucharist is the most power-filled thing anyone could ever do. The Eucharist empowers ministers. If you call on God, God will be there, and it will frighten the hell out of you.

NOTES

1. Resident Aliens Among Us

1. Max Stackhouse, Princeton Theological Seminary, "Liberalism Dispatched vs. Liberalism Engaged," *The Christian Century* (October 18, 1995): 962.
2. Rebekah Miles-Deloney, The Divinity School, The University of Chicago, review in *Quarterly Review* (Winter 1990): 104.
3. Nibs Stroupe, *Journal for Preachers* 14, 1 (1990): 36-37.
4. Leander E. Keck, Yale Divinity School, *The Church Confident* (Nashville: Abingdon Press, 1993), p. 76.

2. Interpreting the Present Time

1. David C. Hester, Professor of Christian Education, Louisville Presbyterian Theological Seminary, review in *Journal of Religious Education* (Spring 1991).
2. William Stringfellow, "St. Ann's-in-the-Sea," in *A Keeper of the Word: Selected Writings of William Stringfellow*, ed. Bill Wylie Kellermann (Grand Rapids: Eerdmans, 1994), p. 154.
3. Rowan Williams, *The Truce of God* (New York: Pilgrim Press, 1983), p. 28.
4. Raymond E. Brown, *The Gospel According to St. John*, Anchor Bible 29 and 29a (Garden City, N.Y.: Doubleday, 1970), p. 1078.

3. Church and World

1. Karl Barth, *The Faith of the Church* (New York: Scribner's, 1959), p. 145.
2. Miroslav Volf, *Ex Auditu* 10 (1994): 15-30.
3. Ibid., p. 28.
4. Max Stackhouse, *The Christian Century* (October 18, 1995): 964.
5. Nicholas Lash, *Believing Three Ways in One God: A Reading of the Apostles' Creed* (South Bend: University of Notre Dame Press, 1993), p. 118.
6. Bonnie Shullenberger, *The Living Church* (May 13, 1990): 10-11.

4. Practice Discipleship

1. Ernst Troeltsch, *The Social Teachings of the Christian Churches*, vol. 2, trans. Olive Wyon (London: Allen & Unwin, 1931), p. 994.
2. John Milbank, *Theology and Social Theology: Beyond Secular Reason* (Oxford: Blackwell, 1990), pp. 111-21.
3. Douglas Sloan, *Faith and Knowledge: Mainline Protestantism and American Higher Education* (Louisville: Westminster/John Knox Press, 1994), p. xx.
4. George Marsden, *The Soul of the American University* (New York: Oxford University Press, 1994).
5. Thomas E. Ricks, *The Wall Street Journal*, Thursday, July 27, 1995.
6. Alasdair MacIntyre, *After Virtue* (South Bend: University of Notre Dame Press, 1984), p. 187.
7. Interview of Stanley Hauerwas by Neil Alexander, *Cokesbury Good Books Catalog* (Fall/Winter 1992–93).

5. Disciplines of Discipleship

1. Walker Percy, *The Message in the Bottle* (New York: Farrar, Straus, and Giroux, 1975), pp. 3-8.

2. Douglas Coupland, *Life After God* (New York: Pocket Books, 1994), p. 305.

3. John S. McClure, *The Four Codes of Preaching* (Philadelphia: Fortress Press, 1991), p. 165.

4. Clifford Elliot is a minister emeritus of Bloor Street United Church, Toronto, and he wrote the piece for the *Toronto Star*.

5. Richard Heitzenrater, *Wesley and the People Called Methodists* (Nashville: Abingdon Press, 1995), p. 192.

6. Ibid., p. 138.

7. Ibid., p. 321.

8. Carl F. H. Henry, "The Church in the World or the World in the Church," *Journal of the Evangelical Theological Society* 34, 3 (1991):381-83.

9. *The Door* (May/June 1993): 249-64.

INDEX

NAMES

SCRIPTURES

SELECTED CHRISTIAN PRACTICES